Selected Poems, 1968–1996

JOSEPH BRODSKY

EDITED BY ANN KJELLBERG

Joseph Brodsky (1940–1996) came to the United States in 1972 as an involuntary exile from the Soviet Union. He received the Nobel Prize in Literature in 1987 and served as poet laureate of the United States in 1991 and 1992. He was the author of three books of poems in English, six books of poems in Russian, and three books of essays in English.

Ann Kjellberg is the literary executor of Joseph Brodsky.

JOSEPH BRODSKY

Selected Poems, 1968–1996

EDITED BY ANN KJELLBERG

WITH TRANSLATIONS FROM THE RUSSIAN BY

Jonathan Aaron, Paul Graves, Anthony Hecht,

George L. Kline, Jane Ann Miller, Howard Moss,

Alan Myers, Derek Walcott, Daniel Weissbort,

and Richard Wilbur

FARRAR, STRAUS AND GIROUX

NEW YORK

Farrar, Straus and Giroux
120 Broadway, New York 10271

Printed in the United States of America
First edition, 2020

Library of Congress Control Number: 2019055650
ISBN: 978-0-374-60036-5

Designed by Gretchen Achilles

Our books may be purchased in bulk for promotional, educational,
or business use. Please contact your local bookseller or the Macmillan
Corporate and Premium Sales Department at 1-800-221-7945, extension 5442,
or by e-mail at MacmillanSpecialMarkets@macmillan.com.

www.fsgbooks.com
www.twitter.com/fsgbooks • www.facebook.com/fsgbooks

1 3 5 7 9 10 8 6 4 2

CONTENTS

INTRODUCTION

by Ann Kjellberg

When Joseph Brodsky got off the plane in Ann Arbor, Michigan, in 1972, at the age of thirty-two, imported by his friend, the Russian professor and basement publisher of censored writers Carl Proffer, who had fetched him from Vienna—the Leningrad authorities had dispatched Brodsky there in an effort to clean house ahead of an expected visit by Richard Nixon—he already had a head full of poetry in English, and of American movies and jazz, Italian painting and architecture, Greek and Roman mythology, and on and on. Although a steady diet of Soviet conformity and canned ideology had driven him from school in Leningrad while he was still a teenager, and an aversion to acquiescence had bumped him through a series of menial jobs and paycheck-pursuing junkets, ultimately landing him in compulsory internal exile in a remote farming village in the subarctic district of Arkhangelsk (for the crime of being, as a poet, technically unemployed), he had for years harbored a slow-burning, private vocation as a reader. His father preserved the ziggurat of books and bookshelves and accumulated literary artifacts with which he walled himself off from the rest of his family's *kommunalka* (communal apartment) in order to read and write into the night, conveying the jumble intact to friends who, with the lifting of Soviet censorship in the 1990s, passed it into various archives where it lingers now.

Brodsky shared this abundance of reading—as wide around the world and as deep into the past as he could go within the constraints of Soviet publishing of the time—with his peers, a generation of young Russian intellectuals peeking warily over the edge of the war's ruins, hungering for art and knowledge and experience to press against the "trimming of the self" demanded by the State. They hand-typed forbidden books with multiple carbons and squinted at them through the dark glass of translations that had barely squeaked in by way of Poland. Brodsky writes of his peers:

> This generation was among the most bookish in the history of Russia, and thank God for that . . . It started as an ordinary accumulation of knowledge but soon became our most important occupation, to which everything could be sacrificed. Books became the first and only reality, whereas reality itself was regarded as either nonsense or nuisance. Compared to others, we were ostensibly flunking or faking our lives. But come to think of it, existence which ignores the standards professed in literature is inferior and unworthy of effort. So we thought, and I think we were right.

Amid this tumult of curiosity and aspiration, pursued in relentless reading, in late-night kitchen disputations, with stealthily befriended foreign students and travelers, by lamplight in the countryside, one realization was coming into focus: young Brodsky was a prodigy in the composition of verse. Russian poetry at the time was relatively green by European standards; its forms had stabilized in the nineteenth century, when most of the Russian elite spoke French. The charmed generation of Russian poets who corresponded to the

English and European Romantics—most famously Pushkin but also the surrounding constellation that Brodsky anthologized in a short handbook for beginners, *An Age Ago* (1988)—were pioneers who had the advantage of plowing fresh ground. While English Victorian poets like Tennyson and Browning were sounding a weary and self-conscious note, their Russian counterparts were still within view of their poetry's beginnings, and their engagement with its formal devices remained fresh.

The Russian language had additional advantages feeding the vitality of its poetic means: Russian is a highly inflected language, so word order is variable, and its system of internal stresses is much more flexible than that of English, allowing for more variety in patterns of rhyme and meter. When Brodsky's immediate predecessors, like Boris Pasternak, Osip Mandelstam, Anna Akhmatova, and Marina Tsvetaeva, were struggling with the murderous violence of the Russian Revolution, they looked to the resources of Russian prosody as a repository of universal and civilized values. To compose in classical measures was an expression of solidarity with a continuous tradition of artistic expression, and of solidarity with worldwide aesthetic ideals against the enforced pragmatism of Soviet ideology. Brodsky writes, "Russian poetry has set an example of moral purity and firmness, which to no small degree has been reflected in the preservation of so-called classical forms," and

> verse meters in themselves are kinds of spiritual magnitudes for which nothing can be substituted. They cannot be replaced even by each other, let alone by free verse. Differences in meters are differences in breath and in heartbeat. Differences in rhyming pattern are those of brain functions.

A poem was more than its semantic meaning: "Poetry amounts to arranging words with the greatest specific gravity in the most effective and externally inevitable sequence . . . It is language negating its own mass and the laws of gravity; it is language's striving upward—or sideways—to that beginning where the Word was," aspiring to its "highest form of existence." The mnemonic power of musicality in verse was inseparable from poetry's force, an awareness magnified by the fact that certain poems existed for these readers only because they had been memorized.

Into this picture Brodsky—self-educated, intense, impulsive, unmoored—emerged as a poetic virtuoso; he did things with Russian verse that no one had thought possible. His mentor, Anna Akhmatova, revered for having asserted her poetic autonomy even when threatened with death and imprisonment, immediately pronounced him the carrier of the embers of Russian verse, dooming him to unwavering attention from the authorities. Others of this cohort, precisely because their commitment was to art, had proved themselves quite ungovernable and were continually in the crosshairs of the State.

Brodsky took a medium, formal poetry—capable of high lyricism, polished to an imperial shine by the wryly skeptical Pushkin and his circle, molded to the agonies of war and oppression by Akhmatova and her generation—and lashed it to a modern sensibility. His idiom embraced classical poise, biblical gravitas, philosophical disenchantment, and street slang. In his little nest in the *kommunalka*, he searched the world for models and peers, coming to rest on English as a needed counterweight: a tonality that was quotidian and antihysterical, a mighty tradition cradled in a gentle landscape. He wrote early poems eulogizing T. S. Eliot and John Donne. But it was in the simple farmhouse of his exile in the far north, where a friend sent him Oscar Williams's *New Pocket Anthology of American Verse*, that he forged during long nights of reading his two most enduring poetic kinships: with W. H. Auden and Robert Frost. He assimilated their practice, using poetic form to undermine grandiose effects, to access a more chastened, open-eyed humanity, into a lifelong poetic position. He later wrote of Auden, "The way he handled the line was telling, at least to me: something like 'Don't cry wolf' even though the wolf's at the door. (Even though, I would add, it looks exactly like you. Especially because of that, don't cry wolf.)"

When Brodsky left Russia as an involuntary exile, he at first feared that, severed from the daily encounter with spoken Russian, he would not write another poem. His vector had in a sense been inevitably international—in another direction, he had always yearned for Italy, the grandeur of its classical proportions and fragmented inheritance—but history dictated that his passage from home be one-way. In the event, within moments of his arrival as a rather improvisatory literature professor at the University of Michigan, he embraced the American demotic and became a presence in American poetry, offering a riposte to the anti-intellectualism and colloquialism of the 1970s and a revitalizing assurance of the ascendancy of art in a society that often associated learning with elitism. The Brodsky who arrived with one suitcase in Ann Arbor in 1972 was nobody's establishment.

Brodsky confronted the situation of exile as an amplification of the existential charge that motored his sensibility. He was a poet of absolute awareness, who had no patience with consolations. To be lonely, to miss your family, your friends, your love, your language, your streets, your known sensations, was to be thrown into the reality of the solitude that is the universe's message. His exile took his twin themes of travel and time and fused them: the past is a place to which you cannot return; the future is a place of infinite emptiness. His love for Italy, where the past is everywhere around you, offered a glimpse of refuge, most poignantly expressed in the comprehensive elegy "Vertumnus," where art is "some loose / silver with which, occasionally, rich infinity / showers the temporary" and where "a sellout-resistant soul / acquires before our eyes the status / of a classic." If his task, and his poetry, became more difficult, it was because it was driven to a more difficult truth. Only in his very last poems does the possibility of home and arrival flicker on the horizon.

Brodsky wrote four books of poetry in Russian while in America (he published in exile two books of poems written previously and censored). The first book in English that he was able to oversee as author, *A Part of Speech* (1980), was an elaborate symphony of collaboration. Editors at Farrar, Straus and Giroux secured literal versions of many of the poems and sent these to the poets with whom Brodsky felt the greatest affinity—Derek Walcott, Richard Wilbur, Anthony Hecht, Howard Moss—who rendered them in an English that Brodsky subsequently, with his own growing command, more and less recast. Other translations were the product of long negotiation. By the time of *To Urania* (1988), Brodsky was taking a greater hand in the proceedings. His approach to his poetry in English has come under fire. He used to reply that his Russian critics (often Soviet) leveled similar complaints—that he forced the outcome, that he overran conventional uses of language, that he was dissonant. I'd advise readers to consider this analogy and dispel the enforcer within—Brodsky's English may challenge the reader's ear in ways that invoke unfamiliar powers in poetry and reward the challenge.

In 1983 Brodsky wrote the essay "To Please a Shadow," in which he describes buying a Latin-font typewriter in order to close the distance between him and his beloved Auden. Proffer had taken Brodsky to visit Auden when he landed in Vienna at the moment of his exile, an encounter that punctuated an internal dialogue that remained unceasing. Brodsky used to quip that he was a Russian poet, an English essayist, and an American citizen. His English essays, published in two volumes in his lifetime as *Less Than One* and *On Grief and Reason*, in addition to a long prose reflection on Venice called *Watermark* and some scattered uncollected pieces, offer a window into a restless mind in which the converging vectors of English and Russian are constantly unfolding, viewed through the atmospheres of still other languages and milieus.

We now live in a time of which Brodsky was an advance scout—a time when many writers operate beyond their original borders and outside their mother tongues, often, like Brodsky, bearing witness to violence and disruption, often answering, through art, to those experiences, in language refracted, by necessity, through other language. In Brodsky's moment there was a cluster of poets, some from the margins of empire, some, like Brodsky, severed from their roots—Walcott, Heaney, Paz, Milosz, to name a few—who brought with them commanding traditions, as well as the imprint of history's dislocations. We would do well now to attend to their song, standing as they did in our doorway between a broken past and the language's future.

A NOTE ON THE TEXT

This book follows the texts established for *Collected Poems in English* (2000), and readers are referred to that volume for annotation and bibliographic information. Where no translator is given, Brodsky composed the poem in English. He prefaced his first book, *A Part of Speech*, with thanks to Ann Frydman, Masha Vorobiova, and Stephen White for preparing interlinear versions of his poems, and thanked Jonathan Aaron, Nancy Meiselas, Margo Picken, David Rieff, Pat Strachan, Peter Viereck, and, "above all," Barry Rubin and Derek Walcott, "for their suggestions, proofreading, and assistance with certain references." He noted, "I have taken the liberty of reworking some of the translations to bring them closer to the original, though perhaps at the expense of their smoothness. I am doubly grateful to the translators for their indulgence."

Selected Poems,

1968–1996

SIX YEARS LATER

So long had life together been that now
the second of January fell again
on Tuesday, making her astonished brow
lift like a windshield wiper in the rain,
    so that her misty sadness cleared, and showed
    a cloudless distance waiting up the road.

So long had life together been that once
the snow began to fall, it seemed unending;
that, lest the flakes should make her eyelids wince,
I'd shield them with my hand, and they, pretending
    not to believe that cherishing of eyes,
    would beat against my palm like butterflies.

So alien had all novelty become
that sleep's entanglements would put to shame
whatever depths the analysts might plumb;
that when my lips blew out the candle flame,
    her lips, fluttering from my shoulder, sought
    to join my own, without another thought.

So long had life together been that all
that tattered brood of papered roses went,
and a whole birch grove grew upon the wall,
and we had money, by some accident,
    and tonguelike on the sea, for thirty days,
    the sunset threatened Turkey with its blaze.

So long had life together been without
books, chairs, utensils—only that ancient bed—
that the triangle, before it came about,
had been a perpendicular, the head
    of some acquaintance hovering above
    two points which had been coalesced by love.

So long had life together been that she
and I, with our joint shadows, had composed
a double door, a door which, even if we
were lost in work or sleep, was always closed:
    somehow its halves were split and we went right
    through them into the future, into night.

Translated by Richard Wilbur

I SIT BY THE WINDOW

FOR LEV LOSEFF

I said fate plays a game without a score,
and who needs fish if you've got caviar?
The triumph of the Gothic style would come to pass
and turn you on—no need for coke, or grass.
    I sit by the window. Outside, an aspen.
    When I loved, I loved deeply. It wasn't often.

I said the forest's only part of a tree.
Who needs the whole girl if you've got her knee?
Sick of the dust raised by the modern era,
the Russian eye would rest on an Estonian spire.
    I sit by the window. The dishes are done.
    I was happy here. But I won't be again.

I wrote: The bulb looks at the floor in fear,
and love, as an act, lacks a verb; the zer-
o Euclid thought the vanishing point became
wasn't math—it was the nothingness of Time.
    I sit by the window. And while I sit
    my youth comes back. Sometimes I'd smile. Or spit.

I said that the leaf may destroy the bud;
what's fertile falls in fallow soil—a dud;
that on the flat field, the unshadowed plain
nature spills the seeds of trees in vain.
    I sit by the window. Hands lock my knees.
    My heavy shadow's my squat company.

My song was out of tune, my voice was cracked,
but at least no chorus can ever sing it back.
That talk like this reaps no reward bewilders
no one—no one's legs rest on my shoulders.
　　I sit by the window in the dark. Like an express,
　　the waves behind the wavelike curtain crash.

A loyal subject of these second-rate years,
I proudly admit that my finest ideas
are second-rate, and may the future take them
as trophies of my struggle against suffocation.
　　I sit in the dark. And it would be hard to figure out
　　which is worse: the dark inside, or the darkness out.

1971

Translated by Howard Moss

LITHUANIAN DIVERTISSEMENT

FOR TOMAS VENCLOVA

I *Introduction*

A modest little country by the sea.
It has its snow, an airport, telephones,
its Jews. A tyrant's brownstone villa.
A statue of a bard is there as well,
who once compared his country to his girlfriend.

The simile displayed, if not good taste,
sound geography: for here the southerners
make Saturday the day to go up north,
from whence, a little drunk, on foot,
they have been known to stray into the West—
a good theme for a sketch. Here distances
are well designed to suit hermaphrodites.

Noonday in springtime. Puddles, banked-up clouds,
stout, countless angels on the gables
of countless churches. Here a man
becomes a victim of a jostling crowd,
or a detail of the homemade baroque.

II *Liejyklos*

To be born a century ago
and over the down bedding, airing,
through a window see a garden grow
and Catherine's crosses, twin domes soaring;
be embarrassed for Mother, hiccup

when the brandished lorgnettes scrutinize
and push a cart with rubbish heaped up
along the ghetto's yellow alleys,
sigh, tucked in bed from head to toe,
for Polish ladies, for example;
and hang around to face the foe
and fall in Poland somewhere, trampled—
for Faith, Tsar, Homeland, or if not,
then shape Jews' ringlets into sideburns
and off, on to the New World like a shot,
puking in waves as the engine churns.

III   *Café Neringa*

Time departs in Vilnius through a café door
accompanied by sounds of clinking forks and spoons,
while Space screws up its eyes from booze the night before
and stares at Time's slowly retreating spine.

A crimson circle, with its far side off,
now hangs moored in utter stillness over roof tiles
and the Adam's apple sharpens, quite as if
the whole face had shrunk to its sheer profile.

Obeying commands like Aladdin's lamp,
a waitress decked out in a cambric halter
saunters about with legs recently clamped
around the neck of a local footballer.

IV *Escutcheon*

St. George, that old dragon slayer,
spear long lost in allegory's glare,
has kept in safety up till now
his sword and steed, and every place
in Lithuania pursues, steadfast,
his aim unheeded by the crowd.

Who now has he, sword clenched in hand,
resolved on taking? What he hounds,
a well-placed coat of arms blots out.
Who can it be? Gentile? Saracen?
The whole world, perhaps? If that's so, then
Vytautas knew well what he was about.

V *Amicum-philosophum de melancholia,*
mania et plica polonica

Sleeplessness. Part of a woman. A glass
replete with reptiles all straining to get out.
The day's long madness has drained across
the cerebellum into the occiput,
forming a pool; one movement and the slush
will feel as if someone, in that icy blot,
has dipped a sharpened quill that, after a pause,
deliberately traces the verb "hate"
in oscillating scribbles to reverse
the brain-wave pattern. Something lipsticked stuffs

the ear with lacerating lengthy words,
like running fingers through a hairdo stiff
with lice. Alone and naked in your sack,
you lie there, fallen from the zodiac.

VI   *Palanga*

Only the sea has power to peer *en face*
at the sky; and a traveler in the dunes
lowers his eyes and sips at his metal flask
like a king in exile, with no psalm-like tunes.

His house ransacked, flocks driven to foreign land.
Son hidden by shepherds inside a cave.
And before him lies just a hem of sand
but his faith's not enough for a walk on waves.

VII   *The Dominicans*

Turn off the thoroughfare, then into
a half-blind street, and once inside
the church, which at this hour is empty,
sit on a bench, adjust your sight,
and, afterwards, in God's whorled ear,
closed to the clash of day's discord,
whisper four syllables, soft and clear:
Forgive me, Lord.

1971

Translated by Alan Myers

NATURE MORTE

Verrà la morte e avrà i tuoi occhi.

—CESARE PAVESE

I

People and things crowd in.
Eyes can be bruised and hurt
by people as well as things.
Better to live in the dark.

I sit on a wooden bench
watching the passersby—
sometimes whole families.
I am fed up with the light.

This is a winter month.
First on the calendar.
I shall begin to speak
when I'm fed up with the dark.

II

It's time. I shall now begin.
It makes no difference with what.
Open mouth. It is better to speak,
although I can also be mute.

What then shall I talk about?
Shall I talk about nothingness?
Shall I talk about days, or nights?
Or people? No, only things,

since people will surely die.
All of them. As I shall.
All talk is barren trade.
A writing on the wind's wall.

III

My blood is very cold—
its cold is more withering
than iced-to-the-bottom streams.
People are not my thing.

I hate the look of them.
Grafted to life's great tree,
each face is firmly stuck
and cannot be torn free.

Something the mind abhors
shows in each face and form.
Something like flattery
of persons quite unknown.

IV

Things are more pleasant. Their
outsides are neither good
nor evil. And their insides
reveal neither good nor bad.

The core of things is dry rot.
Dust. A wood borer. And
brittle moth-wings. Thin walls.
Uncomfortable to the hand.

Dust. When you switch lights on,
there's nothing but dust to see.
That's true even if the thing
is sealed up hermetically.

V

This ancient cabinet—
outside as well as in—
strangely reminds me of
Paris's Notre Dame.

Everything's dark within
it. Dust mop or bishop's stole
can't touch the dust of things.
Things themselves, as a rule,

don't try to purge or tame
the dust of their own insides.
Dust is the flesh of time.
Time's very flesh and blood.

VI

Lately I often sleep
during the daytime. My
death, it would seem, is now
trying and testing me,

placing a mirror close
to my still-breathing lips,
seeing if I can stand
non-being in daylight.

I do not move. These two
thighs are like blocks of ice.
Branched veins show blue against
skin that is marble white.

VII

Summing their angles up
as a surprise to us,
things drop away from man's
world—a world made with words.

Things do not move, or stand.
That's our delirium.
Each thing's a space, beyond
which there can be no thing.

A thing can be battered, burned,
gutted, and broken up.
Thrown out. And yet the thing
never will yell, "Oh, fuck!"

VIII

A tree. Its shadow, and
earth, pierced by clinging roots.
Interlaced monograms.
Clay and a clutch of rocks.

Roots interweave and blend.
Stones have their private mass
which frees them from the bond
of normal rootedness.

This stone is fixed. One can't
move it, or heave it out.
Tree shadows catch a man,
like a fish, in their net.

IX

A thing. Its brown color. Its
blurry outline. Twilight.
Now there is nothing left.
Only a *nature morte*.

Death will come and will find
a body whose silent peace
will reflect death's approach
like any woman's face.

Scythe, skull, and skeleton—
an absurd pack of lies.
Rather: "Death, when it comes,
will have your own two eyes."

X

Mary now speaks to Christ:
"Are you my son?—or God?
You are nailed to the cross.
Where lies my homeward road?

"Can I pass through my gate
not having understood:
Are you dead?—or alive?
Are you my son?—or God?"

Christ speaks to her in turn:
"Whether dead or alive,
woman, it's all the same—
son or God, I am thine."

1971
Translated by George L. Kline

THE FUNERAL OF BOBÒ

I

Bobò is dead, but don't take off your hat.
No gesture we could make will help us bear it.
Why mount a butterfly upon the spit
of the Admiralty tower? We'd only tear it.

On every side, no matter where you glance,
are squares of windows. As for "What happened?"—well,
open an empty can by way of answer,
and say, "Just that, as near as one can tell."

Bobò is dead. Wednesday is almost over.
On streets which offer you no place to go,
such whiteness lies. Only the night river,
with its black water, does not wear the snow.

II

Bobò is dead; there's sadness in this line.
O window squares, O arches' semicircles,
and such fierce frost that if one's to be slain,
let blazing firearms do the dirty work.

Farewell, Bobò, my beautiful and sweet.
These teardrops dot the page like holes in cheese.
We are too weak to follow you, and yet
to take a stand exceeds our energies.

Your image, as I here and now predict,
whether in crackling cold or waves of heat,
shall never dwindle—quite the reverse, in fact—
in Rossi's matchless, long, and tapering street.

III

Bobò is dead. Something I might convey
slips from my grasp, as bath soap sometimes does.
Today, within a dream, I seemed to lie
upon my bed. And there, in fact, I was.

Tear off a page, but read the date aright:
it's with a zero that our woes commence.
Without her, dreams suggest the waking state,
and squares of air push through the window vents.

Bobò is dead. One feels an impulse, with
half-parted lips, to murmur "Why? What for?"
It's emptiness, no doubt, which follows death.
That's likelier than hell—and worse, what's more.

IV

You were all things, Bobò. But your decease
has changed you. You are nothing; you are not;
or, rather, you are a clot of emptiness—
which also, come to think of it, is a lot.

Bobò is dead. To these round eyes, the view
of the bare horizon line is like a knife.
But neither Kiki nor Zazà, Bobò,
will ever take your place. Not on your life.

Now Thursday. I believe in emptiness.
There, it's like hell, but shittier, I've heard.
And the new Dante, pregnant with his message,
bends to the empty page and writes a word.

1972

Translated by Richard Wilbur

NUNC DIMITTIS

When Mary first came to present the Christ Child
to God in his temple, she found—of those few
who fasted and prayed there, departing not from it—
    devout Simeon and the prophetess Anna.

The holy man took the babe up in his arms.
The three of them, lost in the grayness of dawn,
now stood like a small shifting frame that surrounded
    the child in the palpable dark of the temple.

The temple enclosed them in forests of stone.
Its lofty vaults stooped as though trying to cloak
the prophetess Anna, and Simeon, and Mary—
    to hide them from men and to hide them from heaven.

And only a chance ray of light struck the hair
of that sleeping infant, who stirred but as yet
was conscious of nothing and blew drowsy bubbles;
    old Simeon's arms held him like a stout cradle.

It had been revealed to this upright old man
that he would not die until his eyes had seen
the Son of the Lord. And it thus came to pass. And
    he said: "Now, O Lord, lettest thou thy poor servant,

according to thy holy word, leave in peace,
for mine eyes have witnessed thine offspring: he is
thy continuation and also the source of
    thy light for idolatrous tribes, and the glory

of Israel as well." Then old Simeon paused.
The silence, regaining the temple's clear space,
oozed from all its corners and almost engulfed them,
    and only his echoing words grazed the rafters,

to spin for a moment, with faint rustling sounds,
high over their heads in the tall temple's vaults,
akin to a bird that can soar, yet that cannot
    return to the earth, even if it should want to.

A strangeness engulfed them. The silence now seemed
as strange as the words of old Simeon's speech.
And Mary, confused and bewildered, said nothing—
    so strange had his words been. He added, while turning

directly to Mary: "Behold, in this child,
now close to thy breast, is concealed the great fall
of many, the great elevation of others,
    a subject of strife and a source of dissension,

and that very steel which will torture his flesh
shall pierce through thine own soul as well. And that wound
will show to thee, Mary, as in a new vision
    what lies hidden, deep in the hearts of all people."

He ended and moved toward the temple's great door.
Old Anna, bent down with the weight of her years,
and Mary, now stooping, gazed after him, silent.
    He moved and grew smaller, in size and in meaning,

to these two frail women who stood in the gloom.
As though driven on by the force of their looks,
he strode through the cold empty space of the temple
    and moved toward the whitening blur of the doorway.

The stride of his old legs was steady and firm.
When Anna's voice sounded behind him, he slowed
his step for a moment. But she was not calling
    to him; she had started to bless God and praise Him.

The door came still closer. The wind stirred his robe
and fanned at his forehead; the roar of the street,
exploding in life by the door of the temple,
    beat stubbornly into old Simeon's hearing.

He went forth to die. It was not the loud din
of streets that he faced when he flung the door wide,
but rather the deaf-and-dumb fields of death's kingdom.
    He strode through a space that was no longer solid.

The rustle of time ebbed away in his ears.
And Simeon's soul held the form of the child—
its feathery crown now enveloped in glory—
    aloft, like a torch, pressing back the black shadows,

to light up the path that leads into death's realm,
where never before until this present hour
had any man managed to lighten his pathway.
    The old man's torch glowed and the pathway grew wider.

FEBRUARY 16, 1972

Translated by George L. Kline

An autumn evening in the modest square
of a small town proud to have made the atlas
(some frenzy drove that poor mapmaker witless,
or else he had the daughter of the mayor).

Here Space appears unnerved by its own feats
and glad to drop the burden of its greatness—
to shrink to the dimensions of Main Street;
and Time, chilled to its bone, stares at the clockface
above the general store, whose crowded shelves
hold every item that this world produces,
from fancy amateur stargazers' tel-
escopes to common pins for common uses.

A movie theater, a few saloons,
around the bend a café with drawn shutters,
a red-brick bank topped with spread-eagle plumes,
a church, whose net—to fish for men—now flutters
unfilled, and which would be paid little heed,
except that it stands next to the post office.
And if parishioners should cease to breed,
the pastor would start christening their autos.

Grasshoppers, in the silence, run amok.
By 6 p.m. the city streets are empty,
unpeopled as if by a nuclear strike.
Just surfacing, the moon swims to the center
of this black window square, like some Eccles-
iastes, glowering; while on the lonely
highway, from time to time, a Buick beams
its blinding headlights at the Unknown Soldier.

The dreams you dream are not of girls half nude
but of your name on an arriving letter.
A morning milkman, seeing milk that's soured,
will be the first to guess that you have died here.
Here you can live, ignoring calendars,
gulp Bromo, never leave the house; just settle
and stare at your reflection in the glass,
as streetlamps stare at theirs in shrinking puddles.

1972

Translated by George L. Kline

IN THE LAKE DISTRICT

In those days, in a place where dentists thrive
(their daughters order fancy clothes from London;
their painted forceps hold aloft on signboards
a common and abstracted Wisdom Tooth),
there I—whose mouth held ruins more abject
than any Parthenon—a spy, a spearhead
for some fifth column of a rotting culture
(my cover was a lit. professorship),
was living at a college near the most
renowned of the fresh-water lakes; the function
to which I'd been appointed was to wear out
the patience of the ingenuous local youth.

Whatever I wrote then was incomplete:
my lines expired in strings of dots. Collapsing,
I dropped, still fully dressed, upon my bed.
At night I stared up at the darkened ceiling
until I saw a shooting star, which then,
conforming to the laws of self-combustion,
would flash—before I'd even made a wish—
across my cheek and down onto my pillow.

1972, ANN ARBOR
Translated by George L. Kline

THE BUTTERFLY

I

Should I say that you're dead?
You touched so brief a fragment
of time. There's much that's sad in
the joke God played.
I scarcely comprehend
the words "you've lived"; the date of
your birth and when you faded
in my cupped hand
and one, and not two dates.
Thus calculated,
your term is, simply stated,
less than a day.

II

It's clear that days for us
are nothings, zeros.
They can't be pinned down near us
to feed our eyes.
Whenever days stand stark
against white borders,
since they possess no bodies,
they leave no mark.
They are like you. That is,
each butterfly's small plumage
is one day's shrunken image—
a tenth its size.

III

Should I say that, somehow,
you lack all being?
What, then, are my hands feeling
that's so like you?
Such colors can't be drawn
from nonexistence.
Tell me, at whose insistence
were yours laid on?
Since I'm a mumbling heap
of words, not pigments,
how could your hues be fragments
of my conceit?

IV

There are, on your small wings,
black spots and splashes—
like eyes, birds, girls, eyelashes.
But of what things
are you the airy norm?
What bits of faces,
what broken times and places
shine through your form?
As for your *nature morte*s;
do they show dishes
of fruits and flowers, or fishes
displayed on boards?

V

Perhaps a landscape smokes
among your ashes,
and with thick reading glasses
I'll scan its slopes—
its beaches, dancers, nymphs.
Is it as bright as
the day, or dark as night is?
And could one glimpse—
ascending that sky's screen—
some blazing lantern?
And tell me, please, what pattern
inspired this scene?

VI

It seems to me you are
a protean creature,
whose markings mask a feature
of face, or stone, or star.
Who was the jeweler,
brow uncontracted,
who from our world extracted
your miniature—
a world where madness brings
us low, and lower,
where we are things, while you are
the thought of things?

VII

Why were these lovely shapes
and colors given
for your one day of life in
this land of lakes?
—a land whose dappled mir-
rors have one merit:
reflecting space, they store it.
Such brief existence tore
away your chance
to be captured, delivered,
within cupped hands to quiver—
the hunter's eye entrance.

VIII

You shun every response—
but not from shyness
or wickedness or slyness,
and not because
you're dead. Dead or alive,
to God's least creature
is given voice for speech, or
for song—a sign
that it has found a way
to bind together,
and stretch life's limits, whether
an hour or day.

IX

But you lack even this:
the means to utter
a word. Yet, probe the matter;
it's better thus.
You're not in heaven's debt,
on heaven's ledger.
It's not a curse, I pledge you,
that your small weight
and span rob you of tongue.
Sound's burden, too, is grievous.
And you're more speechless,
less fleshed, than time.

X

Living too brief an hour
for fear or trembling,
you spin, motelike, ascending
above this bed of flowers,
beyond the prison space
where past and future
combine to break, or batter,
our lives, and thus
when your path leads you far
to open meadows,
your pulsing wings bring shadows
and shapes to air.

XI

So, too, the sliding pen
which inks a surface
has no sense of the purpose
of any line
or that the whole will end
as an amalgam
of heresy and wisdom;
it therefore trusts the hand
whose silent speech incites
fingers to throbbing—
whose spasm reaps no pollen,
but eases hearts.

XII

Such beauty, set beside
so brief a season,
suggests to our stunned reason
this bleak surmise:
the world was made to hold
no end or *telos*,
and if—as some would tell us—
there is a goal,
it's not ourselves.
No butterfly collector
can trap light or detect where
the darkness dwells.

XIII

Should I bid you farewell
as to a day that's over?
Men's memories may wither,
grow thin, and fall
like hair. The trouble is,
behind their backs are:
not double beds for lovers,
hard sleep, the past,
or days in shrinking files
backstretched—but, rather,
huge clouds, circling together,
of butterflies.

XIV

You're better than No-thing.
That is, you're nearer,
more reachable, and clearer.
Yet you're akin
to nothingness—
like it, you're wholly empty.
And if, in your life's venture,
No-thing takes flesh,
that flesh will die.
Yet while you live you offer
a frail and shifting buffer,
dividing it from me.

1973 • *Translated by George L. Kline*

LAGOON

FOR BROOKE AND STROBE TALBOTT

I

Down in the lobby three elderly women, bored,
take up, with their knitting, the Passion of Our Lord
    as the universe and the tiny realm
of the *pension* Accademia, side by side,
with TV blaring, sail into Christmastide,
    a lookout desk clerk at the helm.

II

And a nameless lodger, a nobody, boards the boat,
a bottle of grappa concealed in his raincoat
    as he gains his shadowy room, bereaved
of memory, homeland, son, with only the noise
of distant forests to grieve for his former joys,
    if anyone is grieved.

III

Venetian church bells, teacups, mantel clocks
chime and confound themselves in this stale box
    of assorted lives. The brazen, coiled
octopus-chandelier appears to be licking,
in a triptych mirror, bedsheet and mattress ticking,
    sodden with tears and passion-soiled.

IV

Blown by night winds, an Adriatic tide
floods the canals, boats rock from side to side,
    moored cradles, and the humble bream,
not ass and oxen, guards the rented bed
where the window blind above your sleeping head
    moves to the sea star's guiding beam.

V

So this is how we cope, putting out the heat
of grappa with nightstand water, carving the meat
    of flounder instead of Christmas roast,
so that Thy earliest backboned ancestor
might feed and nourish us, O Savior,
    this winter night on a damp coast.

VI

A Christmas without snow, tinsel, or tree,
at the edge of a map- and land-corseted sea;
    having scuttled and sunk its scallop shell,
concealing its face while flaunting its backside,
Time rises from the goddess's frothy tide,
    yet changes nothing but clock hand and bell.

VII

A drowning city, where suddenly the dry
light of reason dissolves in the moisture of the eye;
    its winged lion, which can read and write,
southern kin of northern sphinxes of renown,
won't drop his book and holler, but calmly drown
    in splinters of mirror, splashing light.

VIII

The gondola knocks against its moorings. Sound
cancels itself, hearing and words are drowned,
    as is that nation where among
forests of hands the tyrant of the State
is voted in, its only candidate,
    and spit goes ice-cold on the tongue.

IX

So let us place the left paw, sheathing its claws,
in the crook of the arm of the other one, because
    this makes a hammer-and-sickle sign
with which to salute our era and bestow
a mute up-yours-even-unto-the-elbow
    upon the nightmares of our time.

X

The raincoated figure is settling into place
where Sophia, Constance, Prudence, Faith, and Grace
    lack futures, the only tense that is
is present, where either a goyish or Yiddish kiss
tastes bitter, like the city, where footsteps fade
    invisibly along the colonnade,

XI

trackless and blank as a gondola's passage through
a water surface, smoothing out of view
    the measured wrinkles of its path,
unmarked as a broad "So long!" like the wide piazza's space,
or as a cramped "I love," like the narrow alleyways,
    erased and without aftermath.

XII

Moldings and carvings, palaces and flights
of stairs. Look up: the lion smiles from heights
    of a tower wrapped as in a coat
of wind, unbudged, determined not to yield,
like a rank weed at the edge of a plowed field,
    and girdled round by Time's deep moat.

XIII

Night in St. Mark's piazza. A face as creased
as a finger from its fettering ring released,
    biting a nail, is gazing high
into that *nowhere* of pure thought, where sight
is baffled by the bandages of night,
    serene, beyond the naked eye,

XIV

where, past all boundaries and all predicates,
black, white, or colorless, vague, volatile states,
    something, some object, comes to mind.
Perhaps a body. In our dim days and few,
the speed of light equals a fleeting view,
    even when blackout robs us blind.

1973

Translated by Anthony Hecht

I was born and grew up in the Baltic marshland
by zinc-gray breakers that always marched on
in twos. Hence all rhymes, hence that wan flat voice
that ripples between them like hair still moist,
if it ripples at all. Propped on a pallid elbow,
the helix picks out of them no sea rumble
but a clap of canvas, of shutters, of hands, a kettle
on the burner, boiling—lastly, the seagull's metal
cry. What keeps hearts from falseness in this flat region
is that there is nowhere to hide and plenty of room for vision.
Only sound needs echo and dreads its lack.
A glance is accustomed to no glance back.

The North buckles metal, glass it won't harm;
teaches the throat to say, "Let me in."
I was raised by the cold that, to warm my palm,
gathered my fingers around a pen.

Freezing, I see the red sun that sets
behind oceans, and there is no soul
in sight. Either my heel slips on ice, or the globe itself
arches sharply under my sole.

And in my throat, where a boring tale
or tea, or laughter should be the norm,
snow grows all the louder and "Farewell!"
darkens like Scott wrapped in a polar storm.

From nowhere with love the enth of Marchember sir
sweetie respected darling but in the end
it's irrelevant who for memory won't restore
features not yours and no one's devoted friend
greets you from this fifth last part of earth
resting on whalelike backs of cowherding boys
I loved you better than angels and Him Himself
and am farther off due to that from you than I am from both
of them now late at night in the sleeping vale
in the little township up to its doorknobs in
snow writhing upon the stale
sheets for the whole matter's skin-
deep I'm howling "youuu" through my pillow dike
many seas away that are milling nearer
with my limbs in the dark playing your double like
an insanity-stricken mirror.

A list of some observations. In a corner, it's warm.
A glance leaves an imprint on anything it's dwelt on.
Water is glass's most public form.
Man is more frightening than his skeleton.
A nowhere winter evening with wine. A black
porch resists an osier's stiff assaults.
Fixed on an elbow, the body bulks
like a glacier's debris, a moraine of sorts.
A millennium hence, they'll no doubt expose
a fossil bivalve propped behind this gauze
cloth, with the print of lips under the print of fringe,
mumbling "Good night" to a window hinge.

I recognize this wind battering the limp grass
that submits to it as they did to the Tartar mass.
I recognize this leaf splayed in the roadside mud
like a prince empurpled in his own blood.
Fanning wet arrows that blow aslant
the cheek of a wooden hut in another land,
autumn tells, like geese by their flying call,
a tear by its face. And as I roll
my eyes to the ceiling, I chant herein
not the lay of that eager man's campaign
but utter your Kazakh name which till now was stored
in my throat as a password into the Horde.

A navy-blue dawn in a frosted pane
recalls yellow streetlamps in the snow-piled lane,
icy pathways, crossroads, drifts on either hand,
a jostling cloakroom in Europe's eastern end.
"Hannibal . . ." drones on there, a worn-out motor,
parallel bars in the gym reek with armpit odor;
as for that scary blackboard you failed to see through,
it has stayed just as black. And its reverse side, too.
Silvery hoarfrost has transformed the rattling bell
into crystal. As regards all that parallel-
line stuff, it's turned out true and bone-clad, indeed.
Don't want to get up now. And never did.

You've forgotten that village lost in the rows and rows
of swamp in a pine-wooded territory where no scarecrows
ever stand in orchards: the crops aren't worth it,
and the roads are also just ditches and brushwood surface.
Old Nastasia is dead, I take it, and Pesterev, too, for sure,
and if not, he's sitting drunk in the cellar or
is making something out of the headboard of our bed:
a wicket gate, say, or some kind of shed.
And in winter they're chopping wood, and turnips is all they live on,
and a star blinks from all the smoke in the frosty heaven,
and no bride in chintz at the window, but dust's gray craft,
plus the emptiness where once we loved.

In the little town out of which death sprawled over the classroom map
the cobblestones shine like scales that coat a carp,
on the secular chestnut tree melting candles hang,
and a cast-iron lion pines for a good harangue.
Through the much-laundered, pale window gauze
woundlike carnations and *kirchen* needles ooze;
a tram rattles far off, as in days of yore,
but no one gets off at the stadium anymore.
The real end of the war is a sweet blonde's frock
across a Viennese armchair's fragile back
while the humming winged silver bullets fly,
taking lives southward, in mid-July.

MUNICH

As for the stars, they are always on.
That is, one appears, then others adorn the inklike
sphere. That's the best way from there to look upon
here: well after hours, blinking.
The sky looks better when they are off.
Though, with them, the conquest of space is quicker.
Provided you haven't got to move
from the bare veranda and squeaking rocker.
As one spacecraft pilot has said, his face
half sunk in the shadow, it seems there is
no life anywhere, and a thoughtful gaze
can be rested on none of these.

Near the ocean, by candlelight. Scattered farms,
fields overrun with sorrel, lucerne, and clover.
Toward nightfall, the body, like Shiva, grows extra arms
reaching out yearningly to a lover.
A mouse rustles through grass. An owl drops down.
Suddenly creaking rafters expand a second.
One sleeps more soundly in a wooden town,
since you dream these days only of things that happened.
There's a smell of fresh fish. An armchair's profile
is glued to the wall. The gauze is too limp to bulk at
the slightest breeze. And a ray of the moon, meanwhile,
draws up the tide like a slipping blanket.

The Laocoön of a tree, casting the mountain weight
off his shoulders, wraps them in an immense
cloud. From a promontory, wind gushes in. A voice
pitches high, keeping words on a string of sense.
Rain surges down; its ropes twisted into lumps,
lash, like the bather's shoulders, the naked backs of these
hills. The Medhibernian Sea stirs round colonnaded stumps
like a salt tongue behind broken teeth.
The heart, however grown savage, still beats for two.
Every good boy deserves fingers to indicate
that beyond today there is always a static to-
morrow, like a subject's shadowy predicate.

If anything's to be praised, it's most likely how
the west wind becomes the east wind, when a frozen bough
sways leftward, voicing its creaking protests,
and your cough flies across the Great Plains to Dakota's forests.
At noon, shouldering a shotgun, fire at what may well
be a rabbit in snowfields, so that a shell
widens the breach between the pen that puts up these limping
awkward lines and the creature leaving
real tracks in the white. On occasion the head combines
its existence with that of a hand, not to fetch more lines
but to cup an ear under the pouring slur
of their common voice. Like a new centaur.

There is always a possibility left—to let
yourself out to the street whose brown length
will soothe the eye with doorways, the slender forking
of willows, the patchwork puddles, with simply walking.
The hair on my gourd is stirred by a breeze
and the street, in distance, tapering to a V, is
like a face to a chin; and a barking puppy
flies out of a gateway like crumpled paper.
A street. Some houses, let's say,
are better than others. To take one item,
some have richer windows. What's more, if you go insane,
it won't happen, at least, inside them.

. . . and when "the future" is uttered, swarms of mice
rush out of the Russian language and gnaw a piece
of ripened memory which is twice
as hole-ridden as real cheese.
After all these years it hardly matters who
or what stands in the corner, hidden by heavy drapes,
and your mind resounds not with a seraphic "do,"
only their rustle. Life, that no one dares
to appraise, like that gift horse's mouth,
bares its teeth in a grin at each
encounter. What gets left of a man amounts
to a part. To his spoken part. To a part of speech.

Not that I am losing my grip: I am just tired of summer.
You reach for a shirt in a drawer and the day is wasted.
If only winter were here for snow to smother
all these streets, these humans; but first, the blasted
green. I would sleep in my clothes or just pluck a borrowed
book, while what's left of the year's slack rhythm,
like a dog abandoning its blind owner,
crosses the road at the usual zebra. Freedom
is when you forget the spelling of the tyrant's name
and your mouth's saliva is sweeter than Persian pie,
and though your brain is wrung tight as the horn of a ram
nothing drops from your pale-blue eye.

1975-76

Translated by Daniel Weissbort and the author

IN ENGLAND

FOR DIANA AND ALAN MYERS

Brighton Rock

And so you are returning, livid flush of early dusk. The chalk
Sussex rocks fling seaward the smell of dry grass and
a long shadow, like some black useless thing. The rippling
sea hurls landward the roar of the incoming surge and
scraps of ultramarine. From the coupling of the splash of
needless water and needless dark arise, sharply
etched against the sky, spires of churches, sheer
rock faces, these livid summer dusks, the color
of landed fish; and I revive. In the bushes, a careless
linnet cries. The horizon's clean-cut clothesline
has a single cloud pegged out upon it, like a shirt,
and a tanker's masts dip and sway, like an ant
fallen over on its back. Into my mind floats someone's
phone number—the ripped-out mesh
of an empty trawl. A breeze fans my cheek.
The sea swell lulls an anxious splinter,
and a motionless boat lies awash in its reflection.
In the middle of a long or at the end of a short
life, one goes down to the waves not to bathe but for the sake
of that dark-gray, unpeopled, inhuman surface,
as like in color to the eyes, gazing unwinking at it,
as two drops of water. Like silence at a parrot.

East Finchley

Evening. A bulky body moves quietly along a narrow
walk, with brush-cut hedges and rows of fuchsias
and geraniums, like a dreadnought on a country canal.
His right jacket sleeve, heavily chalk-dusted, betrays
the way he makes his living, as does his very voice:
"You can get away with watering roses and gladioli
somewhat less than dahlias or hyacinths—once or
twice a week." And he quotes me figures from
The Amateur Gardener's Handbook
and a line from Virgil. The ground swallows the water
with unexpected haste, and he hides his eyes. In the living room,
sparely furnished, deliberately bare,
his wife—he's been married twice—as befits wives,
lays out, humming, John Galsworthy's favorite patience,
"Spider." On the wall a watercolor: in a river
a bridge is reflected, who knows where.

Anyone living on an island is aware that sooner
or later all this ends: the water in the tap
ceases to be fresh, tastes salty; the foot,
crunching through the gravel and straw, senses
a sudden chill inside the toe end of the boot.
In music there's that place when the record
starts to spin against the moving needle.
On the mantelpiece a stuffed quail looms
that once relied on an infinity of forest,

a vase with a sprig of silver birch,
and a postcard of an Algerian bazaar: heaps
of multicolored stuffs, bronze vessels,
camels somewhere at the back—or is it hills?—
men in turbans. Not like us.

An allegory of memory, embodied in a hard
pencil poised in the air above the crossword.
A house, on a deserted street laid out on a slope,
in whose identical windows the setting sun
reflects as if on those of an express train
heading for an eternity where wheels are not required.
The sweet bedroom (a doll between the pillows)
where she has her "nightmares." The kitchen,
where the gas ring's humming chrysanthemum gives out
the smell of tea. And the outlines of the body
sink into an armchair the way sediment settles in liquid.
Amid the absurdity, horror, ennui of life,
beyond the windows stand the flowers, like tiny
apparel somehow inside out—a rose, symbol
of infinity with its clustered eights,
a dahlia's wheel, spinning between its bamboo bars
like Boccioni's disheveled locomotive,
fuchsia dancers, and, not yet fully open,
irises. Floating in peace, a world
where no one asks, "What's that? What did you say?
Would you repeat that?"—for here the echo

sends the word back unfailingly to the ear
even from as far as the Chinese Wall. Because you
uttered just one word: "Flowers."

Soho

A massive Venetian mirror holds the opaque profile
of a silk-robed beauty with the crimson wound
of a soundless mouth. The listener scans the walls,
whose pattern has altered over eight years to "Scenes
at Epsom Races." Flags. A jockey in scarlet cap
flies to the winning post on a two-year-old
colt. All merge into one great blur. The stands
go berserk. ". . . didn't reply to my
second letter, so I decided . . ." The voice
is, as it were, a struggle between the verb
and the absent tense. The young, thin hand
ripples the locks that are flowing, falling
into nowhere, like many rivers'
waters. Presently straddling oaken
stallions, two who have fallen heroically in foreign
sheets gallop round the table with its unfinished
bottle toward the gate in what's-it
street. Flags droop down, the wind dies, and drops
of moisture gleam on a rider's lips,
and the stands simply vanish . . . A yellow lamp
burns by the gate, slightly gilding the snowdrifts like
the crumbling crust on a Viennese pastry. No matter who

gets here first, though, in this street the bell
doesn't ring and the hoofs of the gray or the bay
in the present past, even reaching the post, leave no
traces, like carousel horses, on real snow.

Three Knights

In the old abbey chancel, in the apse, on the floor,
three knights sleep their last sleep, gleaming
in the chancel's gloom like stone sturgeon,
scales of chain mail, armor-plate gills. All three
hawk-nosed and hatchet-faced, head-to-heel
knights: in breastplate, helmet, long sword. And sleep
longer than they woke. Dusk in the chancel. Arms
crossed on the chest, like carps.

The flash follows the camera's click—a kind
of shot (anything that hurls us forward
onto the wall of the future's a shot). The three,
frozen still, enact once again within
the camera what has already taken place—at Poitiers,
or the Holy Land: a traveler in a straw hat is,
for those who died for Father, Son,
and Holy Ghost, more fearful than the Saracen.

The abbey sprawled at ease along the riverbank.
Clumps of green trees. White butterflies
flutter over flower beds by the chapter house.

The cool of an English noonday. In England, as nowhere else,
nature, rather than diverting, soothes the eye;
and under the chancel wall, as if before
a theater curtain lowered once and for all,
the hawthorn's applause singles out none of them with its call.

North Kensington

The rustle of an *Irish Times* harried by the wind along
railway tracks to a depot long abandoned,
the crackle of dead wormwood, heralding autumn,
a gray tongue of water close by gums of brick.
How I love these sounds—the sounds of aimless
but continuing life, which for long enough
have been sufficient, aside from the crunch of
my own weighty tread on the gravel. And I fling a bolt skyward.
Only a mouse comprehends the delights of waste ground—
a rusting rail, discarded metal pins,
slack wire, reduced to a husky C-sharp,
the defeat of time in the face of metal.
All beyond repair, no further use.
You can only asphalt it over or blast
it clean off the face of the earth, used by now
to grimacing concrete stadia and their bawling crowds.
Then the mouse will come. Slowly, no rush,
out into the middle of the field, tiny as the soul
is in relation to the flesh, and, raising its
little snout, aghast, will shriek, "What is this place?"

York: In Memoriam W. H. Auden

The butterflies of northern England dance above the goosefoot
below the brick wall of a dead factory. After Wednesday
comes Thursday, and so on. The sky breathes heat;
the fields burn. The towns give off a smell of striped
cloth, long-wrapped and musty; dahlias die of thirst.
And your voice—"I have known three great poets. Each
one a prize son of a bitch"—sounds in my ears
with disturbing clarity. I slow my steps

and turn to look round. Four years soon
since you died in an Austrian hotel. Under the crossing sign
not a soul: tiled roofs, asphalt, limestone,
poplars. Chester died, too—you know that
only too well. Like beads on a dusty abacus,
sparrows sit solemnly on wires. Nothing so much
transforms a familiar entrance into a crowd of columns
as love for a man, especially when

he's dead. The absence of wind compels taut leaves
to tense their muscles and stir against their will.
The white butterflies' dance is like a storm-tossed ship.
A man takes his own blind alley with him wherever he goes
about the world; and a bent knee, with its obtuse angle,
multiplies the captive perspective,
like a wedge of cranes holding their course
for the south. Like all things moving onward.

The emptiness, swallowing sunlight—something in common with
the hawthorn—grows steadily more palpable
in the outstretched hand's direction, and
the world merges into a long street where others live.
In this sense, it is England. England, in this sense,
still an empire and fully capable—if
you believe the music gurgling like water—
of ruling waves. Or any element, for that matter.

Lately, I've been losing my grip a little: snarl
at my shopwindow reflection; while my finger
dials its number, my hand lets the phone fall.
Closing my eyes, I see an empty boat,
motionless, far out in the bay.
Coming out of the phone booth,
I hear a starling's voice—in its cry alarm.
But before it flies away the sound

melts in the air. Whose blue expanse, innocent of objects,
is much like this life here (where things stand out more in the desert),
for you're not here. And vacuum gradually
fills the landscape. Like flecks of foam,
sheep take their ease on bottle-green waves
of Yorkshire heather. The corps de ballet of nimble
butterflies, taking their cue from an unseen bow,
flicker above a grass-grown ditch, giving the eye

no point of rest. And the willow herb's vertical stalk
is longer than the ancient Roman road,
heading north, forgotten by all at Rome.
Subtracting the greater from the lesser—time from man—
you get words, the remainder, standing out against their
white background more clearly than the body
ever manages to while it lives, though it cry "Catch me!"—

thus the source of love turns into the object of love.

Stone Villages

The stone-built villages of England.
A cathedral bottled in a pub window.
Cows dispersed across the fields.
Monuments to kings.

A man in a moth-eaten suit
sees a train off, heading, like everything here, for the sea,
smiles at his daughter, leaving for the East.
A whistle blows.

And the endless sky over the tiles
grows bluer as swelling birdsong fills.
And the clearer the song is heard,
the smaller the bird.

1976 • *Translated by Alan Myers*

PLATO ELABORATED

I

I should like, Fortunatus, to live in a city where a riv-
er would jut out from under a bridge like a hand from a sleeve,
      and would flow toward the gulf, spreading its fingers
like Chopin, who never shook a fist at anyone as long as he lived.

There would be an Opera House, in which a slightly overripe
tenor would duly descant Mario's arias, keep-
      ing the Tyrant amused. He'd applaud from his loge, but
I from the back rows would hiss through clenched teeth, "You creep."

That city would not lack a yacht club, would not lack
a soccer club. Noting the absence of smoke from the brick
      factory chimneys, I'd know it was Sunday,
and would lurch in a bus across town, clutching a couple of bucks.

I'd twine my voice into the common animal hoot-
ing on that field where what the head begins is finished by the foot.
      Of the myriad laws laid down by Hammurabi
the most important deal with corner kicks, and penalty kicks to boot.

II

I'd want a Library there, and in its empty halls I'd browse
through books containing precisely the same number of commas as
      the dirty words in daily gutter language—
words which haven't yet broken into literary prose. Much less into
      verse.

There'd be a large Railroad Station in that city—its façade,
damaged in war, would be much more impressive than the outside
       world. Spotting a palm tree in an airline window,
the ape that dozes within me would open its two eyes wide.

And when winter, Fortunatus, threw its coarse shroud over the
       square,
I would wander, yawning, through the Gallery, where
       every canvas, especially those of David and Ingres,
would seem as familiar as any birthmarks are.

From my window, at dusk, I would watch the horde
of bleating automobiles as they flash back and forth
       past shapely nude columns in Doric hairdos,
standing pale and unrebellious on the steps of the City Court.

III

There would be a café in that city with a quite
decent blancmange, where, if I should ask why
       we need the twentieth century when we already
have the nineteenth, my colleague would stare fixedly at his fork or
       his knife.

Surely there is a street in that city with twin rows of trees,
an entranceway flanked by a nymph's torso, and other things equally
    recherchés:
        and a portrait would hang in the drawing room, giving you an
            idea
of how the mistress of the house looked in her salad days.

I would hear an unruffled voice calmly treat
of things not related to dinner by candlelight;
    the flickering flames on the hearth, Fortunatus,
would splash crimson stains on a green dress. But finally the fire
    would go out.

Time, which—unlike water—flows horizontally, threading its way
from Friday to Saturday, say,
    would, in the dark of that city, smooth out every wrinkle
and then, in the end, wash its own tracks away.

IV

And there ought to be monuments there. Not only the bronze riders
    I would know by name—
men who have thrust their feet into History's stirrups to tame
    History—I would know the names of the stallions also,
considering the stamp which the latter came

to brand the inhabitants with. A cigarette glued
to my lip, walking home well past midnight, I would conjecture
    aloud—
        like some gypsy parsing an open palm, between hiccups,
reading the cracks in the asphalt—what fate the lifeline of the city
    showed.

And when they would finally arrest me for espionage,
for subversive activity, vagrancy, for *ménage*
        à trois, and the crowd, boiling around me, would bellow,
poking me with their work-roughened forefingers, "Outsider! We'll
    settle your hash!"—

then I would secretly smile, and say to myself, "See,
this is your chance to find out, in Act Three,
        how it looks from the inside—you've stared long enough at
        the outside—
so take note of every detail as you shout, '*Vive la Patrie!*'"

1977

Translated by George L. Kline

LETTERS FROM THE MING DYNASTY

I

Soon it will be thirteen years since the nightingale
fluttered out of its cage and vanished. And, at nightfall,
the Emperor washes down his medicine with the blood
of another tailor, then, propped on silk pillows, turns on a jeweled bird
that lulls him with its level, identical song.
It's this sort of anniversary, odd-numbered, wrong,
that we celebrate these days in our "Land-under-Heaven."
The special mirror that smooths wrinkles even
costs more every year. Our small garden is choked with weeds.
The sky, too, is pierced by spires like pins in the shoulder blades
of someone so sick that his back is all we're allowed to see,
and whenever I talk about astronomy
to the Emperor's son, he begins to joke . . .
This letter to you, Beloved, from your Wild Duck
is brushed onto scented rice paper given me by the Empress.
Lately there is no rice but the flow of rice paper is endless.

II

"A thousand-li-long road starts with the first step," as
the proverb goes. Pity the road home does
not depend on that same step. It exceeds ten times
a thousand li, especially counting from zeros.
One thousand li, two thousand li—
a thousand means "Thou shalt not ever see
thy native place." And the meaninglessness, like a plague,
spreads from words onto numbers, onto zeros especially.

Wind blows us westward like the yellow tares
from a dried pod, there where the Wall towers.
Against it man's figure is ugly and stiff as a frightening hieroglyph,
as any illegible scripture at which one stares.
This pull in one direction only has made
me something elongated, like a horse's head,
and all the body should do is spent by its shadow
rustling across the wild barley's withered blade.

1977
Translated by Derek Walcott

MAY 24, 1980

I have braved, for want of wild beasts, steel cages,
carved my term and nickname on bunks and rafters,
lived by the sea, flashed aces in an oasis,
dined with the-devil-knows-whom, in tails, on truffles.
From the height of a glacier I beheld half a world, the earthly
width. Twice have drowned, thrice let knives rake my nitty-gritty.
Quit the country that bore and nursed me.
Those who forgot me would make a city.
I have waded the steppes that saw yelling Huns in saddles,
worn the clothes nowadays back in fashion in every quarter,
planted rye, tarred the roofs of pigsties and stables,
guzzled everything save dry water.
I've admitted the sentries' third eye into my wet and foul
dreams. Munched the bread of exile: it's stale and warty.
Granted my lungs all sounds except the howl;
switched to a whisper. Now I am forty.
What should I say about my life? That it's long and abhors
     transparence.
Broken eggs make me grieve; the omelette, though, makes me vomit.
Yet until brown clay has been crammed down my larynx,
only gratitude will be gushing from it.

1980
Translated by the author

A POLAR EXPLORER

All the huskies are eaten. There is no space
left in the diary. And the beads of quick
words scatter over his spouse's sepia-shaded face
adding the date in question like a mole to her lovely cheek.
Next, the snapshot of his sister. He doesn't spare his kin:
what's been reached is the highest possible latitude!
And, like the silk stocking of a burlesque half-nude
queen, it climbs up his thigh: gangrene.

1977
Translated by the author

A hotel in whose ledgers departures are more prominent than arrivals.
With wet Koh-i-noors the October rain
strokes what's left of the naked brain.
In this country laid flat for the sake of rivers,
beer smells of Germany and seagulls are
in the air like a page's soiled corners.
Morning enters the premises with a coroner's
punctuality, puts its ear
to the ribs of a cold radiator, detects sub-zero:
the afterlife has to start somewhere.
Correspondingly, the angelic curls
grow more blond, the skin gains its distant, lordly
white, while the bedding already coils
desperately in the basement laundry.

1981

THE HAWK'S CRY IN AUTUMN

Wind from the northwestern quarter is lifting him high above
the dove-gray, crimson, umber, brown
Connecticut Valley. Far beneath,
chickens daintily pause and move
unseen in the yard of the tumbledown
farmstead, chipmunks blend with the heath.

Now adrift on the airflow, unfurled, alone,
all that he glimpses—the hills' lofty, ragged
ridges, the silver stream that threads
quivering like a living bone
of steel, badly notched with rapids,
the townships like strings of beads

strewn across New England. Having slid down to nil
thermometers—those household gods in niches—
freeze, inhibiting thus the fire
of leaves and churches' spires. Still,
no churches for him. In the windy reaches,
undreamt of by the most righteous choir,

he soars in a cobalt-blue ocean, his beak clamped shut,
his talons clutched tight into his belly
—claws balled up like a sunken fist—
sensing in each wisp of down the thrust
from below, glinting back the berry
of his eyeball, heading south-southeast

to the Rio Grande, the Delta, the beech groves and farther still:
to a nest hidden in the mighty groundswell
of grass whose edges no fingers trust,
sunk amid forest's odors, filled
with splinters of red-speckled eggshell,
with a brother or a sister's ghost.

The heart overgrown with flesh, down, feather, wing,
pulsing at feverish rate, nonstopping,
propelled by internal heat and sense,
the bird goes slashing and scissoring
the autumnal blue, yet by the same swift token,
enlarging it at the expense

of its brownish speck, barely registering on the eye,
a dot, sliding far above the lofty
pine tree; at the expense of the empty look
of that child, arching up at the sky,
that couple that left the car and lifted
their heads, that woman on the stoop.

But the uprush of air is still lifting him
higher and higher. His belly feathers
feel the nibbling cold. Casting a downward gaze,
he sees the horizon growing dim,
he sees, as it were, the features
of the first thirteen colonies whose

chimneys all puff out smoke. Yet it's their total within his sight
that tells the bird of his elevation,
of what altitude he's reached this trip.
What am I doing at such a height?
He senses a mixture of trepidation
and pride. Heeling over a tip

of wing, he plummets down. But the resilient air
bounces him back, winging up to glory,
to the colorless icy plane.
His yellow pupil darts a sudden glare
of rage, that is, a mix of fury
and terror. So once again

he turns and plunges down. But as walls return
rubber balls, as sins send a sinner to faith, or near,
he's driven upward this time as well!
He! whose innards are still so warm!
Still higher! Into some blasted ionosphere!
That astronomically objective hell

of birds that lacks oxygen, and where the milling stars
play millet served from a plate or a crescent.
What, for the bipeds, has always meant
height, for the feathered is the reverse.
Not with his puny brain but with shriveled air sacs
he guesses the truth of it: it's the end.

And at this point he screams. From the hooklike beak
there tears free of him and flies *ad luminem*
the sound Erinyes make to rend
souls: a mechanical, intolerable shriek,
the shriek of steel that devours aluminum;
"mechanical," for it's meant

for nobody, for no living ears:
not man's, not yelping foxes',
not squirrels' hurrying to the ground
from branches; not for tiny field mice whose tears
can't be avenged this way, which forces
them into their burrows. And only hounds

lift up their muzzles. A piercing, high-pitched squeal,
more nightmarish than the D-sharp grinding
of the diamond cutting glass,
slashes the whole sky across. And the world seems to reel
for an instant, shuddering from this rending.
For the warmth burns space in the highest as

badly as some iron fence down here
brands incautious gloveless fingers.
We, standing where we are, exclaim
"There!" and see far above the tear
that is a hawk, and hear the sound that lingers
in wavelets, a spider skein

swelling notes in ripples across the blue vault of space
whose lack of echo spells, especially in October,
an apotheosis of pure sound.
And caught in this heavenly patterned lace,
starlike, spangled with hoarfrost powder,
silver-clad, crystal-bound,

the bird sails to the zenith, to the dark-blue high
of azure. Through binoculars we foretoken
him, a glittering dot, a pearl.
We hear something ring out in the sky,
like some family crockery being broken,
slowly falling aswirl,

yet its shards, as they reach our palms, don't hurt
but melt when handled. And in a twinkling
once more one makes out curls, eyelets, strings,
rainbowlike, multicolored, blurred
commas, ellipses, spirals, linking
heads of barley, concentric rings—

the bright doodling pattern the feather once possessed,
a map, now a mere heap of flying
pale flakes that make a green slope appear
white. And the children, laughing and brightly dressed,
swarm out of doors to catch them, crying
with a loud shout in English, "Winter's here!"

1975 • *Translated by Alan Myers with the author*

SEXTET

I

An eyelid is twitching. From the open mouth
gushes silence. The cities of Europe mount
each other at railroad stations. A pleasant odor
of soap tells the jungle dweller of the approaching foe.
Wherever you set your sole or toe,
the world map develops blank spots, grows balder.

A palate goes dry. The traveler's seized by thirst.
Children, to whom the worst
should be done, fill the air with their shrieks. An eyelid twitches
all the time. As for columns, from
the thick of them someone always emerges. Even in your sweet
　　　dream,
even with your eyes shut, you see human features.

And it wells up in your throat like barf:
"Give me ink and paper and, as for yourself,
scram!" And an eyelid is twitching. Odd, funereal
whinings—as though someone's praying upstairs—poison the daily
　　　grind.
The monstrosity of what's happening in your mind
makes unfamiliar premises look familiar.

II

Sometimes in the desert you hear a voice. You fetch
a camera in order to catch the face.
But—too dark. Sit down, then, release your hearing
to the Southern lilt of a small monkey who
left her palm tree but, having no leisure to
become a human, went straight to whoring.

Better sail by steamer, horizon's ant,
taking part in geography, in blueness, and
not in history, this dry land's scabies.
Better trek across Greenland on skis and camp
along the icebergs, among the plump
walruses as they bathe their babies.

The alphabet won't allow your trip's goal to be
ever forgotten, that famed point B.
There a crow caws hard, trying to play the raven;
there a black sheep bleats, rye is choked with weeds;
there the top brass, like furriers, shear out bits
of the map's faded pelt, so that they look even.

III

For thirty-six years I've stared at fire.
An eyelid is twitching. Both palms perspire:
the cop leaves the room with your papers. Angst. Built to calm it,
an obelisk, against its will, recedes
in a cloud, amidst bright seeds,
like an immobile comet.

Night. With your hair quite gone, you still dine alone,
being your own grand master, your own black pawn.
The kipper's soiling a headline about striking rickshaws
or a berserk volcano's burps—
God knows where, in other words—
flitting its tail over "The New Restrictions."

I comprehend only the buzz of flies
in the Eastern bazaars! On the sidewalk, flat
on his back, the traveler strains his sinews,
catching the air with his busted gills.
In the afterlife, the pain that kills
here no doubt continues.

IV

"Where's that?" asks the nephew, toying with his stray locks.
And, fingering brown mountain folds, "Here," pokes
the niece. In the depths of the garden, yellow
swings creak softly. The table dwarfs a bouquet
of violets. The sun's splattering the parquet
floor. From the drawing room float twangs of a cello.

At night, a plateau absorbs moonshine.
A boulder shepherds its elephantine
shadow. A brook's silver change is spending
itself in a gully. Clutched sheets in a room elude
their milky/swarthy/abandoned nude—
an anonymous painful painting.

In spring, labor ants build their muddy coops;
rooks show up; so do creatures with other groups
of blood; a fresh leaf shelters
the verging shame of two branches. In autumn, a sky hawk keeps
counting villages' chicklets; and the sahib's
white jacket is dangling from the servant's shoulders.

V

Was the word ever uttered? And then—if yes—
in what language? And where? And how much ice
should be thrown into a glass to halt a *Titanic*
of thought? Does the whole recall the neat shapes of parts?
Would a botanist, suddenly facing birds
in an aquarium, panic?

Now let us imagine an absolute emptiness.
A place without time. The air *per se*. In this,
in that, and in the third direction—pure, simple, pallid
air. A Mecca of it: oxygen, nitrogen. In which
there's really nothing except for the rapid twitch-
ing of a lonely eyelid.

These are the notes of a naturalist. The naughts
on nature's own list. Stained with flowerpots.
A tear falls in a vacuum without acceleration.
The last of hotbed neu-roses, hearing the
faint buzzing of time's tsetse,
I smell increasingly of isolation.

VI

And I dread my petals' joining the crowned knot
of fire! Most resolutely not!
Oh, but to know the place for the first, the second,
and the umpteenth time! When everything comes to light,
when you hear or utter the jewels like
"When I was in the army" or "Change the record!"

Petulant is the soul begging mercy from
an invisible or dilated frame.
Still, if it comes to the point where the blue acrylic
dappled with cirrus suggests the Lord,
say, "Give me strength to sustain the hurt,"
and learn it by heart like a decent lyric.

When you are no more, unlike the rest,
the latter may think of themselves as blessed
with the place so much safer than to the big withdrawal
of what your conscience indeed amassed.
And a fish that prophetically shines with rust
will splash in a pond and repeat your oval.

1976
Translated by the author

ROMAN ELEGIES

TO BENEDETTA CRAVERI

I

The captive mahogany of a private Roman
flat. In the ceiling, a dust-covered crystal island.
At sunset, the windowpanes pan a common
ground for the nebulous and the ironed.
Setting a naked foot on the rosy marble,
the body steps toward its future: to its attire.
If somebody shouted "Freeze!" I'd perform that marvel
as this city happily did in its childhood hour.
The world's made of nakedness and of foldings.
Still, the latter's richer with love than a face, that's certain.
Thus an opera tenor's so sweet to follow
since he yields invariably to a curtain.
By nightfall, a blue eye employs a tear,
cleansing, to a needless shine, the iris;
and the moon overhead apes an emptied square
with no fountain in it. But of rock as porous.

II

The month of stalled pendulums. Only a fly in August
in a dry carafe's throat is droning its busy hymn.
The numerals on the clock face crisscross like earnest
antiaircraft searchlights probing for seraphim.
The month of drawn blinds, of furniture wrapped in cotton
shrouds, of the sweating double in the mirror above the cupboard,
of bees that forget the topography of their hives and, coated
with suntan honey, keep staggering seaward.

Get busy then, faucet, over the snow-white, sagging
muscle, tousle the tufts of thin gray singes!
To a homeless torso and its idle, grabby
mitts, there's nothing as dear as the sight of ruins.
And they, in their turn, see themselves in the broken Jewish
r no less gladly: for the pieces fallen
so apart, saliva's the only solution they wish
for, as time's barbarous corneas scan the Forum.

III

The tiled, iron-hot, glowing hills: midsummer.
Clouds feel like angels, thanks to their cooling shadows.
Thus the bold cobblestone eyes, like a happy sinner,
the blue underthings of your leggy blond friend. A bard of
trash, extra thoughts, broken lines, unmanly,
I hide in the bowels of the Eternal City
from the luminary that rolled back so many
marble pupils with rays bright enough for setting
up yet another universe. A yellow square. Noontime's
stupor. A Vespa's owner tortures the screaming gears.
Clutching my chest with my hand, at a distance
I reckon the change from the well-spent years.
And, like a book at once opened to all its pages,
the laurels scratch the scorched white of a balustrade.
And the Colosseum looms, the skull of Argus,
through whose sockets clouds drift like a thought of the vanished herd.

IV

Two young brunettes in the library of the husband
of the more stunning one. Two youthful, tender
ovals hunch over pages: a Muse telling Fate the substance
of several things she tried to render.
The swish of old paper, of red crepe de chine. A humming
fan mixes violets, lavender, and carnations.
Braiding of hair: an elbow thrusts up its summit
accustomed to cumulus-thick formations,
Oh, a dark eye is obviously more fluent
in brown furniture, pomegranates, oak shutters.
It's more keen, it's more cordial than a blue one;
to the blue one, though, nothing matters!
The blue one can always tell the owner
from the goods, especially before closing—
that is, time from living—and turn the latter over,
as tails strain to look at heads in tossing.

V

Jig, little candle tongue, over the empty paper,
bow to the rotten breath as though you were courted,
follow—but don't get too close!—the pauper
letters standing in line to obtain the content.
You animate the walls, wardrobe, the sill's sweetbriar:
more than handwriting is ever after;
even your soot, it appears, soars higher
than the holiest wish of these musings' author.

Still, in their midst you earn yourself a decent
name, as my fountain pen, in memory of your tender
commas, in Rome, at the millennium's end, produces
a lantern, a cresset, a torch, a taper,
never a period—and the premises look their ancient
selves, from the severed head down to a yellow toenail.
For an ink pot glows bright whenever someone mentions
light, especially in a tunnel.

VI

Clicking of a piano at the siesta hour.
Stillness of sleepy mews acquires
C-flats, as scales coat a fish which narrows
round the corner. Exhaling quarrels,
inhaling a fusty noon's air, the stucco
flaps its brown gills, and a sultry, porous
cavity of a mouth scatters
around cold pearls of Horace.
I've never built that cloud-thrusting stony
object that could explain clouds' pallor.
I've learned about my own, and any
fate, from a letter, from its black color.
Thus some fall asleep while hugging
a Leica, in order to take a picture
of the dream, to make themselves out, having
awakened in a developed future.

VII

Eggshells of cupolas, vertebrae of bell towers.
Colonnades' limbs sprawled wide in their blissful, heathen
leisure. The square root of a skylark scours
the bottomless, as though prior to prayers, heaven.
Light reaps much more than it has sown: an awkward
body hides in a crack while its shadow shutters
walls. In these parts, all windows are looking northward,
where the more one boozes the less one matters.
North! A white iceberg's frozen-in piano;
smallpoxed with quartz, vases' granite figures;
a plain unable to stop field-glass scanning;
sweet Ashkenazy's ten running fingers.
Never again are the legions to thread those contours:
to a creaking pen, even its words won't hearken.
And the golden eyebrow—as, at sunset, a cornice—
rises up, and the eyes of the darling darken.

VIII

In these squinting alleyways, where even a thought about
one's self is too cumbersome, in this furrowed clutter
of the brain which has long since refused to cloud
the universe, where now keyed up, now scattered,
you trundle your boots on the cobbled, checkered
squares, from a fountain and back to a Caesar—
thus a needle shuffles across the record
skipping its grooves—it is altogether

proper to settle now for a measly fraction
of remaining life, for the past life craving
completeness, for its attempts to fashion
an integer. The sound the heels are scraping
from the ground is the aria of their union,
a serenade that what-has-been-longer
hums to what's-to-be-shorter. This is a genuine
Caruso for a gramophone-dodging mongrel.

IX

Lesbia, Julia, Cynthia, Livia, Michelina.
Bosoms, ringlets of fleece: for effects, and for causes also.
Heaven-baked clay, fingertips' brave arena.
Flesh that renders eternity an anonymous torso.
You breed immortals: those who have seen you bare,
they, too, turned Catulluses, statues, heavy
Neros, et cetera. Short-term goddesses! you are
much more a joy to believe in than a permanent bevy.
Hail the smooth abdomen, thighs as their hamstrings tighten.
White upon white, as Kazimir's dream image,
one summer evening, I, the most mortal item
in the midst of this wreckage resembling the whole world's rib cage,
sip with feverish lips wine from a tender collar-
bone; the sky is as pale as a cheek with a mole that trembles;
and the cupolas bulge like the tits of the she-wolf, fallen
asleep after having fed her Romulus and her Remus.

X

Mimicking local pines, embrace the ether!

The fingertips won't cull much more than the pane's tulle quiver.

Still, a little black bird won't return from the sky blue, either.

And we, too, aren't gods in miniature, that's clear.

That's precisely why we are happy: because we are nothings; speckled

pores are spurned by summits or sharp horizons;

the body is space's reversal, no matter how hard you pedal.

And when we are unhappy, it's perhaps for the same small reasons.

Better lean on a portico, loose the white shirt that billows,

stone cools the spinal column, gray pigeons mutter,

and watch how the sun is sinking into gardens and distant villas,

how the water—the tutor

of eloquence—pours from the rusted lips, repeating

not a thing, save a nymph with her marble truants,

save that it's cold and fresh, save that it's splitting

the face into rippling ruins.

XI

Private life. Fears, shredded thoughts, the jagged

blanket renders the contours of Europe meager.

By means of a blue shirt and a rumpled jacket

something still gets reflected in the wardrobe mirror.

Let's have some tea, face, so that the teeth may winnow

lips. Yoked by a ceiling, the air grows flatter.

Cast inadvertently through the window,

a glance makes a bunch of blue jays flutter

from their pine tops. A room in Rome, white paper,
the tail of a freshly drawn letter: a darting rodent.
Thus, thanks to the perfect perspective, some objects peter
out; thus, still others shuffle across the frozen
Tanaïs, dropping from the picture, limping,
occiputs covered with wilted laurels and blizzards' powder—
toward Time, lying beyond the limits
of every spraddling superpower.

XII

Lean over. I'll whisper something to you: I am
grateful for everything: for the chicken cartilage
and for the chirr of scissors already cutting
out the void for me—for it is your hem.
Doesn't matter if it's pitch-black, doesn't matter if
it holds nothing: no ovals, no limbs to count.
The more invisible something is,
the more certain it's been around,
and the more obviously it's everywhere. You
were the first to whom all this happened, were you?
For a nail holding something one would divide by two—
were it not for remainders—there is no gentler quarry.
I was in Rome. I was flooded by light. The way
a splinter can only dream about.
Golden coins on the retina are to stay—
enough to last one through the whole blackout.

1981 • *Translated by the author*

TO URANIA

TO I. K.

Everything has its limit, including sorrow.
A windowpane stalls a stare. Nor does a grill abandon
a leaf. One may rattle the keys, gurgle down a swallow.
Loneliness cubes a man at random.
A camel sniffs at the rail with a resentful nostril;
a perspective cuts emptiness deep and even.
And what is space anyway if not the
body's absence at every given
point? That's why Urania's older than sister Clio!
In daylight or with the soot-rich lantern,
you see the globe's pate free of any bio,
you see she hides nothing, unlike the latter.
There they are, blueberry-laden forests,
rivers where the folk with bare hands catch sturgeon
or the towns in whose soggy phone books
you are starring no longer; farther eastward surge on
brown mountain ranges; wild mares carousing
in tall sedge; the cheekbones get yellower
as they turn numerous. And still farther east, steam dreadnoughts or
    cruisers,
and the expanse grows blue like lace underwear.

1981

Translated by the author

SEVEN STROPHES

I was but what you'd brush
with your palm, what your leaning
brow would hunch to in evening's
raven-black hush.

I was but what your gaze
in that dark could distinguish:
a dim shape to begin with,
later—features, a face.

It was you, on my right,
on my left, with your heated
sighs, who molded my helix,
whispering at my side.

It was you by that black
window's trembling tulle pattern
who laid in my raw cavern
a voice calling you back.

I was practically blind.
You, appearing, then hiding,
gave me my sight and heightened
it. Thus some leave behind

a trace. Thus they make worlds.
Thus, having done so, at random
wastefully they abandon
their work to its whirls.

Thus, prey to speeds
of light, heat, cold, or darkness,
a sphere in space without markers
spins and spins.

1981

Translated by Paul Graves

ECLOGUE IV: WINTER

TO DEREK WALCOTT

Ultima Cumaei venit iam carminis aetas;
magnus ab integro saeclorum nascitur ordo.

—VIRGIL, *Eclogue IV*

I

In winter it darkens the moment lunch is over.
It's hard then to tell starving men from sated.
A yawn keeps a phrase from leaving its cozy lair.
The dry, instant version of light, the opal
snow, dooms tall alders—by having freighted
them—to insomnia, to your glare,

well after midnight. Forget-me-nots and roses
crop up less frequently in dialogues. Dogs with languid
fervor pick up the trail, for they, too, leave traces.
Night, having entered the city, pauses
as in a nursery, finds a baby under the blanket.
And the pen creaks like steps that are someone else's.

II

My life has dragged on. In the recitative of a blizzard
a keen ear picks up the tune of the Ice Age.
Every "Down in the Valley" is, for sure,
a chilled boogie-woogie. A bitter, brittle
cold represents, as it were, a message
to the body of its final temperature

or—the earth itself, sighing out of habit
for its galactic past, its sub-zero horrors.
Cheeks burn crimson like radishes even here.
Cosmic space is always shot through with matte agate,
and the beeping Morse, returning homeward,
finds no ham operator's ear.

III

In February, lilac retreats to osiers.
Imperative to a snowman's profile,
carrots get more expensive. Limited by a brow,
a glance at cold, metallic objects
is fiercer than the metal itself. This, while
you peel eyes from objects, still may allow

no shedding of blood. The Lord, some reckon,
was reviewing His world in this very fashion
on the eighth day and after. In winter, we're
not berry pickers: we stuff the cracks with oakum,
praise the common good with a greater passion,
and things grow older by, say, a year.

IV

In great cold, pavements glaze like a sugar candy,
steam from the mouth suggests a dragon,
if you dream of a door, you tend to slam it.
My life has dragged on. The signs are plenty.
They'd make yet another life, just as dragging.
From these signs alone one would compose a climate

or a landscape. Preferably with no people,
with virgin white through a lacework shroud,
—a world where nobody heard of Parises, Londons; where
weekdays are spun by diffusive, feeble
light; where, too, in the end you shudder
spotting the ski tracks . . . Well, just a pair.

V

Time equals cold. Each body, sooner
or later, falls prey to a telescope. With the years,
it moves away from the luminary, grows colder.
Hoarfrost jungles the windowpane with sumac,
ferns, or horsetail, with what appears
to be nursed on this glass and deprived of color

by loneliness. But, as with a marble hero,
one's eye rolls up rather than runs in winter.
Where sight fails, yielding to dreams' swarmed forces,
time, fallen sharply beneath the zero,
burns your brain like the index finger
of a scamp from popular Russian verses.

VI

My life has dragged on. One cold resembles another
cold. Time looks like time. What sets them apart is only
a warm body. Mule-like, stubborn creature,
it stands firmly between them, rather
like a border guard: stiffened, sternly
preventing the wandering of the future

into the past. In winter, to put it bleakly,
Tuesday is Saturday. The daytime is a deceiver:
Are the lights out already? Or not yet on? It's chilly.
Dailies might as well be printed weekly.
Time stares at a looking glass like a diva
who's forgotten what's on tonight: *Tosca*? Oh no, *Lucia*?

VII

Dreams in the frozen season are longer, keener.
The patchwork quilt and the parquet deal,
on their mutual squares, in chessboard warriors.
The hoarser the blizzard rules the chimney,
the hotter the quest for a pure ideal
of naked flesh in a cotton vortex,

and you dream nasturtiums' stubborn odor,
a tuft of cobwebs shading a corner nightly,
in a narrow ravine torrid Terek's splashes,
a feast of fingertips caught in shoulder
straps. And then all goes quiet. Idly
an ember smolders in dawn's gray ashes.

VIII

Cold values space. Baring no rattling sabers,
it takes hill and dale, townships and hamlets
(the populace cedes without trying
tricks), mostly cities, whose great ensembles,
whose arches and colonnades, in hundreds,
stand like prophets of cold's white triumph,

looming wanly. Cold is gliding
from the sky on a parachute. Each and every column
looks like a fifth, desires an overthrow.
Only the crow doesn't take snow gladly.
And you often hear the angry, solemn,
patriotic gutturals speaking crow.

IX

In February, the later it is, the lower
the mercury. More time means more cold. Stars, scattered
like a smashed thermometer, turn remotest
regions of night into a strep marvel.
In daytime, when sky is akin to stucco,
Malevich himself wouldn't have noticed

them, white on white. That's why angels
are invisible. To their legions
cold is of benefit. We would make them
out, the winged ones, had our eyes' angle
been indeed on high, where they are linking
in white camouflage like Finnish marksmen.

X

For me, other latitudes have no usage.
I am skewered by cold like a grilled goose portion.
Glory to naked birches, to the fir-tree needle,
to the yellow bulb in an empty passage—
glory to everything set by the wind in motion:
at a ripe age, it can replace the cradle.

The North is the honest thing. For it keeps repeating
all your life the same stuff—whispering, in full volume,
in the life dragged on, in all kinds of voices;
and toes freeze numb in your deerskin creepers,
reminding you, as you complete your polar
conquest, of love, of shivering under clock faces.

XI

In great cold, distance won't sing like sirens.
In space, the deepest inhaling hardly
ensures exhaling, nor does departure
a return. Time is the flesh of the silent
cosmos. Where nothing ticks. Even being hurtled
out of the spacecraft, one wouldn't capture

any sounds on the radio—neither fox-trots nor maidens
wailing from a hometown station.
What kills you out there, in orbit, isn't
the lack of oxygen but the abundance
of time in its purest (with no addition
of your life) form. It's hard to breathe it.

XII

Winter! I cherish your bitter flavor
of cranberries, tangerine crescents on faience saucers,
the tea, sugar-frosted almonds (at best, two ounces).
You were opening our small beaks in favor
of names like Marina or Olga—morsels
of tenderness at that age that fancies

cousins. I sing a snowpile's blue contours
at dusk, rustling foil, clicking B-flat somewhere,
as though "Chopsticks" were tried by the Lord's own finger.
And the logs, which rattled in stony courtyards
of the gray, dank city that freezes bare
by the sea, are still warming my every fiber.

XIII

At a certain age, the time of year, the season
coincides with fate. Theirs is a brief affair.
But on days like this you sense you are right. Your worries
about things that haven't come your way are ceasing,
and a simple botanist may take care
of commenting upon daily life and mores.

In this period, eyes lose their green of nettles,
the triangle drops its geometric ardor:
all the angles drawn with cobwebs are fuzzy.
In exchanges on death, place matters
more and more than time. The cold gets harder.
And saliva suddenly burns its cozy

XIV

tongue, like that coin. Still, all the rivers
are ice-locked. You can put on long johns and trousers,
strap steel runners to boots with ropes and a piece of timber.
Teeth, worn out by the tap dance of shivers,
won't rattle because of fear. And the Muse's
voice gains a reticent, private timbre.

That's the birth of an eclogue. Instead of the shepherd's signal,
a lamp's flaring up. Cyrillic, while running witless
on the pad as though to escape the captor,
knows more of the future than the famous sibyl:
of how to darken against the whiteness,
as long as the whiteness lasts. And after.

1977
Translated by the author

THE FLY

TO IRENE AND ALFRED BRENDEL

I

While you were singing, fall arrived.
A splinter set the stove alight.
While you were singing, while you flew,
the cold wind blew.

And now you crawl the flat expanse of
my greasy stove top, never glancing
back to whence you arrived last April,
slow, barely able

to put one foot before the other.
So crushing you would be no bother.
Yet death's more boring to a scholar's eye
than torment, fly.

II

While you were singing, while you flew, the leafage
fell off. And water found it easier
to run down to the ground and stare,
disinterested, back into air.

But your eyesight has gone a bit asunder.
The thought of your brain dimming under
your latticed retina—downtrodden,
matte, tattered, rotten—

unsettles one. Yet you seem quite aware of
and like, in fact, this mildewed air of
well-lived-in quarters, green shades drawn.
Life does drag on.

III

Ah, buggie, you've lost all your perkiness;
you look like some old shot-down Junkers,
like one of those scratched flicks that score
the days of yore.

Weren't you the one who in those times so fatal
droned loud above my midnight cradle,
pursued by crossing searchlights into
my black-framed window?

Yet these days, as my yellowed finger-
nail mindlessly attempts to fiddle
with your soft belly, you won't buzz with fear
or hatred, dear.

IV

While you sang on, the gray outside grew grayer.
Damp door-frame joints swell past repair;
drafts numb the soles. This place of mine
is in decline.

You can't be tempted, though, by the sink's outrageous
slumped pyramids, unwashed for ages,
nor by sweet, shiftless honeymoons
in sugar dunes.

You're in no mood for that. You're in no mood to
take all that sterling-silver crap. Too good to
let yourself in for all that mess.
Me too, I guess.

V

Those feet and wings of yours! they're so old-fashioned,
so quaint. One look at them, and one imagines
a cross between Great-grandma's veil
et la Tour Eiffel

—the nineteenth century, in short. However,
by likening you to this and that, my clever
pen ekes out of your sorry end
a profit and

prods you to turn into some fleshless substance,
thought-like, unpalpable—into an absence
ahead of schedule. Your pursuer
admits: it's cruel.

VI

What is it that you muse of there?
Of your worn-out though uncomputed derring-
do orbits? Of six-legged letters,
your printed betters,

your splayed Cyrillic echoes, often
spotted by you in days gone by on open
book pages, and—misprints abhorring—
fast you'd be soaring

off. Now, though, since your eyesight lessens,
you spurn those black-on-white curls, tresses,
releasing them to real brunettes, their ruffles,
chignons, thick afros.

VII

While you were singing, while you flew, the birds went
away. Brooks, too, meander free, unburdened
of stickleback. Groves flaunt see-throughs—no takers.
The cabbage acres

crackle with cold, though tightly wrapped for winter,
and an alarm clock, like a time bomb, whimpers
tick-tock somewhere; its dial's dim and hollow:
the blast won't follow.

Apart from that, there are no other sounds.
Rooftop by rooftop, light rebounds
back into cloud. The stubble shrivels.
It gives one shivers.

VIII

And here's just two of us, contagion's carriers.
Microbes and sentences respect no barriers,
afflicting all that can inhale or hear.
Just us two here—

your tiny countenance pent up with fear
of dying, my sixteen, or near,
stones playing at some country squire—
plus autumn's mire.

Completely gone, it seems, your precious buzzer.
To time, though, this appears small bother—
to waste itself on us. Be grateful
that it's not hateful,

IX

that it's not squeamish. Or that it won't care
what sort of shoddy deal, what kind of fare
it's getting stuck with in the guise of
some large nose-divers

or petty ones. Your flying days are over.
To time, though, ages, sizes never
appear distinguishable. And it poses
alike for causes

as for effects, by definition. Even—
nay! notably—if those are given
in miniature: like to cold fingers,
small change's figures.

X

So while you were off there, busy flirting
around the half-lit lightbulb's flicker,
or, dodging me, amidst the rafters,
it—time—stayed rather

the same as now, when you acquire the stature
—due to your impotence and to your posture
toward myself—of pallid dust. Don't ponder,
decrepit, somber,

that time is my ally, my partner.
Look, we are victims of a common pattern.
I am your cellmate, not your warden.
There is no pardon.

XI

Outside, it's fall. A rotten time for bare
carnelian twigs. Like in the Mongol era,
the gray, short-legged species messes
with yellow masses,

or just makes passes. And yet no one cares
for either one of us. It seems what pairs us
is some paralysis—that is, your virus.
You'd be desirous

to learn how fast one catches this, though lucid,
indifference and sleep-inducing
desire to pay for stuff so global
with its own obol.

XII

Don't die! Resist! Crawl! though you don't feel youthful.
Existence is a bore when useful,
for oneself specially—when it spells a bonus.
A lot more honest

is to hound calendars' dates with a presence
devoid of any sense or reasons,
making a casual observer gather:
life's just another

word for non-being and for breaking rules. Were
you younger, my eyes'd scan the sphere
where all that is abundant. You are,
though, old and near.

XIII

So here's two of us. Outside, rain's flimsy
beak tests the windowpanes, and in a whimsy
crosshatches the landscape: its model.
You are immobile.

Still, there's us two. At least, when you expire,
I mentally will note the dire
event, thus mimicking the loops so boldly
spun by your body

in olden times, when they appeared so witless.
Death too, you know, once it detects a witness,
less firmly puts full-stops, I bet,
than tête-à-tête.

XIV

I hope you're not in pain, just lonely.
Pain takes up space; it therefore could only
creep toward you from outside, sneak near
you from the rear

and cup you fully—which implies, I reckon,
my palm that's rather busy making
these sentences. Don't die as long as
the worst, the lowest

still can be felt, still makes you twitch. Ah, sister!
to hell with the small brain's disaster!
A thing that quits obeying, dammit,
like that stayed moment,

XV
is beautiful in its own right. In other
words, it's entitled to applause (well, rather,
to the reversed burst), to extend its labor.
Fear's but a table

of those dependencies that dryly beckon
one's atrophy to last an extra second.
And I for one, my buzzy buddy,
I am quite ready

to sacrifice one of my own. However,
now such a gesture is an empty favor:
quite shot, my Shiva, is your motor;
your torpor's mortal.

XVI

In memory's deep faults, great vaults, among her
vast treasures—spent, dissolved, disowned or
forgotten (on the whole, no miser
could size them, either

in ancient days or, moreover, later)—
amidst existence's loose change and glitter,
your near-namesake, called the Muse, now makes a
soft bed, dear *Musca*

domestica, for your protracted
rest. Hence these syllables, hence all this prattling,
this alphabet's cortege: ink trailers,
upsurges, failures.

XVII

Outside, it's overcast. Designed for friction
against the furniture, my means of vision
gets firmly trained on the wallpaper.
You're in no shape to

take to the highest its well-traveled pattern,
to stun up there, where prayers pummel
clouds, feeble seraphs with the notion
of repetition

and rhythm—seen senseless in their upper
realms, being rooted in the utter
despair for which these cloudborne insects
possess no instincts.

XVIII

What will it end like? In some housefly heaven?
an apiary or, say, hidden
barn, where above spread cherry jam a heavy
and sleepy bevy

of your ex-sisters slowly twirls, producing
a swish the pavement makes when autumn's using
provincial towns? Yet push the doors:
a pale swarm bursts

right past us back into the world—out! out!—
enveloping it in their white shroud
whose winter-like shreds, snatches, forms
—whose swarm confirms

XIX

(thanks to this flicker, bustling, frantic)
that souls indeed possess a fabric
and matter, and a role in landscape,
where even blackest

things in the end, for all their throttle,
too, change their hue. That the sum total
of souls surpasses any tribe.
That color's time

or else the urge to chase it—quoting
the great Halicarnassian—coating
rooftops *en face*, hills in profile
with its white pile.

XX

Retreating from their pallid whirlwind,
shall I discern you in their winged
(a priori, not just Elysian)
a-swirling legion,

and you swoop down in your familiar fashion
onto my nape, as though you missed your ration
of mush that thinks itself so clever?
Fat chance. However,

having kicked off the very last—by eons—
you'll be the last among those swarming millions.
Yet if you're let in on a scene so private,
then, local climate

XXI

considered—so capricious, flippant—
next spring perhaps I'll spot you flitting
through skies into this region, rushing
back home. I, sloshing

through mud, might sigh, "A star is shooting,"
and vaguely wave to it, assuming
some zodiac mishap—whereas
there, quitting spheres,

that will be your winged soul, a-flurry
to join some dormant larva buried
here in manure, to show its nation
a transformation.

Translated by Jane Ann Miller and the author

IN MEMORIAM

The thought of you is receding like a chambermaid given notice.
No! like a railway platform, with block-lettered DVINSK or TATRAS.
But odd faces loom in, shivering and enormous,
also terrains, only yesterday entered into the atlas,
thus filling up the vacuum. None of us was well suited
for the status of statues. Probably our blood vessels
lacked in hardening lime. "Our family," you'd have put it,
"gave the world no generals, or—count our blessings—
great philosophers." Just as well, though: the Neva's surface
can't afford yet another reflection, brimming with mediogres.
What can remain of a mother with all her saucepans
in the perspective daily extended by her son's progress?
That's why the snow, this poor man's marble, devoid of muscle
        power,
melts, blaming empty brain cells for their not so clever
locks, for their failure to keep the fashion in which you, by putting
        powder
on your cheek, had meant to look forever.
What is left is to shield the skull, with raised arms, against idle
        glances,
and the throat, with the lips' nonstop "She has died, she has died,"
        while endless
cities rip the retinal sacs with lances
clanging loud like returning empties.

1985

Translated by the author

A SONG

I wish you were here, dear,
I wish you were here.
I wish you sat on the sofa
and I sat near.
The handkerchief could be yours,
the tear could be mine, chin-bound.
Though it could be, of course,
the other way around.

I wish you were here, dear,
I wish you were here.
I wish we were in my car,
and you'd shift the gear.
We'd find ourselves elsewhere,
on an unknown shore.
Or else we'd repair
to where we've been before.

I wish you were here, dear,
I wish you were here.
I wish I knew no astronomy
when stars appear,
when the moon skims the water
that sighs and shifts in its slumber.
I wish it were still a quarter
to dial your number.

I wish you were here, dear,
in this hemisphere,
as I sit on the porch
sipping a beer.
It's evening, the sun is setting;
boys shout and gulls are crying.
What's the point of forgetting
if it's followed by dying?

1989

A FOOTNOTE TO WEATHER FORECASTS

A garden alley with statues of hardened mud,
akin to gnarled, stunted tree trunks.
Some of them I knew personally; the rest
I see for the first time ever. Presumably they are gods
of local woods and streams, guardians of silence.
As for the feminine shapes—nymphs and so forth—they look
thought-like, i.e., unfinished;
each one strives to keep, even here,
in the future that came, her vagrant's status.

A chipmunk won't pop up and cross the path.
No birdsong is audible, nor, moreover, a motor.
The future is a panacea
against anything prone to repetition.
And in the sky there are scattered, like a bachelor's
clothes, clouds, turned inside out
or pressed. It smells of conifer—
this prickly substance of not so familiar places.
Sculptures loom in the twilight, darkening
thanks to their proximity to each other, thanks
to the indifference of the surrounding landscape.

Should any one of them speak, you would
sigh rather than gasp or shudder
upon hearing well-known voices, hearing
something like "The child wasn't yours" or "True,
I testified against him, but out of fear,
not jealousy"—petty, twenty-
odd-year-old secrets of purblind hearts
obsessed with a silly quest for power
over their likes. The best ones among them were
at once the executioners and the victims.

It's good that someone else's memories
interfere with your own. It's good that some
of these figures, to you, appear
alien. Their presence hints
at different events, at a different sort of fate—
perhaps not a better one, yet clearly
the one that you missed. This unshackles
memory more than imagination—
not forever, of course, but for a while. To learn
that you've been deceived, that you've been completely
forgotten, or, the other way around,
that you are still being hated
is extremely unpleasant, but to regard yourself
as the hub of even a negligible universe,
unbearable and indecent.

                    A rare,
perhaps the only, visitor to these parts,
I have, I suppose, a right
to describe the observed. Here it is, our little
Valhalla, our long overgrown estate
in time, with a handful of mortgaged souls,
with its meadows where a sharpened sickle
won't roam, in all likelihood, with abandon,
and where snowflakes float in the air as a good example
of poise in a vacuum.

1986

Translated by the author

STAR OF THE NATIVITY

In the cold season, in a locality accustomed to heat more than
to cold, to horizontality more than to a mountain,
a child was born in a cave in order to save the world;
it blew as only in deserts in winter it blows, athwart.

To Him, all things seemed enormous: His mother's breast, the steam
out of the ox's nostrils, Caspar, Balthazar, Melchior—the team
of Magi, their presents heaped by the door, ajar.
He was but a dot, and a dot was the star.

Keenly, without blinking, through pallid, stray
clouds, upon the child in the manger, from far away—
from the depth of the universe, from its opposite end—the star
was looking into the cave. And that was the Father's stare.

DECEMBER 1987

Translated by the author

IN MEMORY OF MY FATHER: AUSTRALIA

You arose—I dreamt so last night—and left for
Australia. The voice, with a triple echo,
ebbed and flowed, complaining about climate,
grime, that the deal with the flat is stymied,
pity it's not downtown, though near the ocean,
no elevator but the bathtub's indeed an option,
ankles keep swelling. "Looks like I've lost my slippers"
came through rapt yet clear via satellite.
And at once the receiver burst into howling *"Adelaide! Adelaide!"*—
into rattling and crackling, as if a shutter,
ripped off its hinges, were pounding the wall with inhuman power.

Still, better this than the silky powder
canned by the crematorium, than the voucher—
better these snatches of voice, this patchwork
monologue of a recluse trying to play a genie

for the first time since you formed a cloud above a chimney.

1989
Translated by the author

EPITAPH FOR A CENTAUR

To say that he was unhappy is either to say too much
or too little: depending on who's the audience.
Still, the smell he'd give off was a bit too odious,
and his canter was also quite hard to match.
He said, They meant just a monument, but something went astray:
the womb? the assembly line? the economy?
Or else, the war never happened, they befriended the enemy,
and he was left as it is, presumably to portray
Intransigence, Incompatibility—that sort of things which proves
not so much one's uniqueness or virtue, but probability.
For years, resembling a cloud, he wandered in olive groves,
marveling at one-leggedness, the mother of immobility.
Learned to lie to himself, and turned it into an art
for want of a better company, also to check his sanity.
And he died fairly young—because his animal part
turned out to be less durable than his humanity.

1988

VERTUMNUS

IN MEMORY OF GIOVANNI BUTTAFAVA

I

I met you the first time ever in latitudes you'd call foreign.
Your foot never trod that loam; your fame, though, had reached
    those quarters
where they fashion the fruit habitually out of plaster.
Knee-deep in snow, you loomed there: white, moreover naked,
in the company of one-legged, equally naked trees,
in your part-time capacity as an expert
on low temperatures. "Roman Deity"
proclaimed a badly faded notice,
and to me you were a deity, since you knew
far more of the past than I (the future
for me in those days was of little import).
On the other hand, apple-cheeked and curly-
haired, you might well have been my agemate; and though you knew
    not a word
of the local dialect, somehow we got to talking.
Initially, I did the chatting. Something about Pomona,
our stubbornly aimless rivers, obstinate foul weather,
the absence of greens and money, leapfrogging seasons
—about things, I thought, that should be up your alley
if not in their essence, then in their common pitch
of lament. Little by little (lament is the universal
ur-tongue; most likely, in the beginning
was either "ouch" or "ai") you began to respond: to squint,
to blink, to furrow your brow; then the lower part of your oval

sort of melted, and your lips were slowly set in motion.
"Vertumnus," you squeezed out finally. "I am called Vertumnus."

II

It was a wintry, pallid—more exactly, a hueless day.
The limbs, the shoulders, the torso—as we proceeded
from subject to subject—were gradually turning pinkish,
and were draped with fabric: a shirt, a jacket, trousers,
a moss-colored coat, shoes from Balenciaga.
The weather got warmer also, and you, at times falling still,
would listen intently into the park's soft rustle,
picking up and examining occasionally a gluey leaf
in your search for just the right word, the right expression.
At any rate, if I am not mistaken,
by the time I, now excessively animated,
was holding forth on history, wars, lousy crops,
brutal government, the lilac had already drooped past its bloom,
and you sat on the bench, from a distance looking
like an average citizen, impoverished by the system;
your temperature was ninety-eight point six.
"Let's go," you muttered, touching me on the elbow.
"Let's go. I'll show you the parts where I was born and grew up."

III

The road there led quite naturally through the clouds,
resembling gypsum in color and, later, marble
so much that it crossed my mind that you had in mind precisely

this: washed-out outlines, chaos, the world in ruins—
though this would have signaled the future, while you already
existed. Shortly afterwards, in an empty
café in a drowsy small town fired white-hot by noon,
where someone who dreamt up an arch just couldn't stop more from
        coming,
I realized I was wrong when I heard you chatting
with some local crone. The language turned out to be
a mix of the evergreen rustle and the ever-blue bubbling of
waves, and so rapid that in the course of the conversation,
you several times, in front of my eyes, turned into
her. "Who is she?" I asked when we ventured out.
"She?" You just shrugged your shoulders. "No one. To you, a
        goddess."

IV

It got a bit colder. We started to chance more often
upon passersby. Some of them would be nodding,
others looked sideways, becoming thus mere profiles.
All of them, however, were noticeably dark-haired.
Each one behind his back had an impeccable perspective,
not excluding the children. As for old men, in their
cases, it coiled like a shell of some snail or other.
Indeed, the past in these parts was much more abundant
than the present! The centuries outnumbered
cars, parked or passing. People and sculpted figures,
as they drew near and as they receded,

neither grew large nor petered out, thus proving
they were, as it were, invariable magnitudes.
It was strange to observe you in your natural circumstances!
Stranger still was the fact that nearly everybody
understood me. This had to do, perhaps,
with the ideal acoustics, caused by the architecture,
or with your intervention—with the basic penchant of an
absolute ear for garbled sounds.
"Don't be surprised. My field is metamorphosis.
Whomsoever I glance at acquires at once my features.
To you, this may come in handy. You are, after all, abroad."

V

A quarter century later I hear your voice, Vertumnus,
uttering these words, and I sense with my skin the steady
stare of your pearl-gray eyes,
odd in a southerner. In the backdrop there are palm trees,
like Chinese characters tousled by the *tramontana*,
and cypresses like Egyptian obelisks.
Noon; a decrepit balustrade somewhere
in Lombardy; and its sun-splattered mortal visage
of a deity! A provisional one for a
deity, but for me the only
one. With widow's peak, with mustachio
(à la Maupassant more than Nietzsche),
with a much thickened—for the sake of disguise, no doubt—
torso. On the other hand, it is not

for me to flash my diameter, to mimic Saturn,
to flirt with a telescope. Everything leaves a spoor,
time especially. Our rings are
those of fat trees with their prospective stump,
not the ones of a rustic round dance in the dooryard,
let alone of a hug. To touch you is to touch a truly
astronomical sum of cells,
which fate always finds affordable, but to which
only tenderness is proportionate.

VI

And I have ensconced myself in the world where your word and
     gesture
were imperative. Mimicry, imitation
were regarded as loyalty. I've mastered the art of merging
with the landscape the way one fades into the furniture or the
     curtains
(which, in the end, influenced my wardrobe).
Now and then in the course of a conversation
the first-person-plural pronoun would start to dribble
off my lips, and my fingers acquired the agility of hedged hawthorn.
Also, I quit glancing back over my padded shoulder. Hearing
footsteps behind me, nowadays I don't tremble:
as previously a chill in my shoulder blades,
nowadays I sense that behind my back also stretches
a street overgrown with colonnades, that at its far end
also shimmer the turquoise crescents

of the Adriatic. Their total is, clearly,
your present, Vertumnus—small change, if you will; some loose
silver with which, occasionally, rich infinity
showers the temporary. Partly out of superstition,
partly, perhaps, because it alone—
the temporary—is capable of sensation,
of happiness. "In this sense, for the likes of me,"
you would squint, "your brethren are useful."

VII

With the passage of years I came almost to the conviction
that the joy of life had become, for you, second nature.
I even started to wonder whether joy is indeed that safe
for a deity. Whether it's not eternity
that a deity pays with in the end for the joy of life.
You'd just brush all this off. But nobody, my Vertumnus,
nobody ever rejoiced so much in the transparent
spurt, in the brick of a basilica, in pine needles,
in wiry handwriting. Much more than we! I even
started to think that you'd gotten infected with
our omnivorousness. Indeed, a view
of a square from a balcony, a clangor of *campanili*,
a streamlined fish, the tattered coloratura
of a bird seen only in profile, laurels'
applause turning into an ovation
—they can be appreciated only by those who do
remember that, come tomorrow, or the day after tomorrow,

all this will end. It's precisely from them, perhaps,
that the immortals learn joy, the knack of smiling
(since the immortals are free from all manner of apprehension).
To the likes of you, in this sense our brethren are useful.

VIII

Nobody ever knew how you were spending nights.
But then that's not strange, taking into consideration
your origins. Once, well past midnight, at the hub of the universe,
I bumped into you, chased by a drove of dimming
stars, and you gave me a wink. Secretiveness? But the cosmos
isn't that secretive. In the cosmos one can see all
things with the naked eye, and they sleep there without blankets.
The intensity of a standard star is such
that its cooling alone can produce an alphabet,
vegetation, sincerity; in the end, ourselves,
with our past, present, future, et cetera—but with the
future especially. We are only
thermometers, brothers and sisters of
ice, not of Betelgeuse. You were made of warmth,
hence your omnipresence. It is difficult to imagine
you in any particular, no matter how shining, dot.
Hence your invisibility. Gods leave no blotches
on a bedsheet, not to mention offspring,
being content with a handmade likeness
in a stony niche, at the end of a garden alley,
happy as a minority; and they are.

IX

An iceberg sails into the tropics. Exhaling smoke, a camel
promotes a pyramid made of concrete, somewhere in the North.
You too, alas, learned to shirk
your immediate duties. To say the least, the four seasons
are more and more one another, eventually getting jumbled
like lire, pounds, dollars, marks, kroner
in a seasoned traveler's wallet.
The papers mutter "greenhouse effect" and "common market,"
but the bones ache at home and overseas alike.
Just look: even that loafer Christo's stone-faced precursor,
which for years used to snake through minefields, is crumbling down.
As a result, birds don't fly away on time
to Africa; characters like myself
less and less often return to the parts they came from;
the rent rises sharply. Apart from having
to exist, one has to pay for that existence monthly.
"The more banal the climate," you once remarked,
"the faster the future becomes the present."

X

On a scorched July dawn, the temperature of a body
plummets, aiming at zero. A horizontal bulk
in the morgue looks like raw material
for garden statuary. Due to a ruptured heart
and immobility. This time around, words
won't do the trick: to you my tongue

is no longer foreign enough to pay
heed to. Besides, one can't
step twice into the same cloud. Even
if you are a god. Especially, if you are not.

XI

In winter the globe sort of shrinks, mentally flattens out.
The latitudes crawl, in twilight especially, upon one another.
The Alps for them are no obstacle. It smells of an ice age,
it smells, I would add, of neolith and of paleolith;
to use the vernacular, of the future. Since
an ice age is a category of the future, which is
that time when finally one loves no one,
even oneself. When you put on clothes
without planning to drop them off all of a sudden
in somebody's parlor. And when you can't walk out into
the street in your blue shirt alone, not to mention naked.
(I've learned quite a bit from you, but not this.) In a certain sense,
the future's got nobody. In a certain sense,
there is nobody in the future that we'd hold dear.
Of course, there are all those moraines and stalagmites everywhere
looming like louvres and skyscrapers with their meltdown contours.
Of course, something moves there: mammoths, mutant
beetles of pure aluminum, some on skis.
But you were a god of subtropics, with the power of supervision
our mixed forests and the black-earth zone—
that birthplace of the past. In the future it has no place,

and you've got nothing to do there. So that's why it crawls in winter
on the foothills of the Alps, on the sweet Apennines, snatching
now a small meadow with its clear brook, now something
plain evergreen: a magnolia, a bunch of laurels;
and not only in winter. The future always
arrives when somebody dies. Especially
if it's a man. Moreover, if it's a god.

XII

A dog painted in bright hues of sunrise
barks at the back of a passerby of midnight color.

XIII

In the past those whom you love don't ever
die. In the past they betray you or peter out into a perspective.
In the past the lapels are narrower, the only pair of loafers
steams by a heater like the ruins of boogie-woogie.
In the past a frozen garden bench
with its surplus of slats resembles
an insane equal sign. In the past the wind
to this day animates the mixture
of Cyrillic and Latin in naked branches:
Ж, Ч, Ш, Щ, plus X, Y, Z,
and your laughter is ringing: "As your head honcho said,
there is nothing that matches abracadabra."

XIV

A quarter century later, a streetcar's broken
vertebrae strike a spark in the evening yonder
as a civic salute to a forever darkened
window. One Caravaggio equals two Bernini,
turning either into a cashmere scarf
or a night at the opera. Now these cited
metamorphoses, left apparently unattended,
continue by pure inertia. Other objects, however, harden
in the condition you left them in,
thanks to which, from now on, they can be afforded by
no one. Display of loyalty? Plain predilection for
monumentality? Or is it simply the brazen future
barging in through the doors, and a sellout-resistant soul
acquires before our eyes the status
of a classic, of solid mahogany, of a Fabergé
egg? Most likely, the latter, which is also a metamorphosis,
and to your credit as well.

                        I've got nothing to plait a wreath with
so as to adorn your cold brow in proper fashion
at the closure of this extraordinarily dry year.
In a tastelessly furnished but large apartment,
like a cur that's suddenly lost its shepherd,
I lower myself onto all fours and scratch
the parquet with my claws, as though underneath were hidden—

because it's from down there that wafts the warmth—
your current existence. At the corridor's distant end
dishes are rattling. Under the tightly shut door the frigid
air thickens, rubbed by incessantly rustling dresses.
"Vertumnus," I whisper, pressing my wet check hard
against yellow floorboards. "Return, Vertumnus."

1990

Translated by the author

TRANSATLANTIC

The last twenty years were good for practically everybody
save the dead. But maybe for them as well.
Maybe the Almighty Himself has turned a bit bourgeois
and uses a credit card. For otherwise time's passage
makes no sense. Hence memories, recollections,
value, deportment. One hopes one hasn't
spent one's mother or father or both, or a handful of friends entirely
as they cease to hound one's dreams. One's dreams,
unlike the city, become less populous
the older one gets. That's why the eternal rest
cancels analysis. The last twenty years were good
for practically everybody and constituted
the afterlife for the dead. Its quality could be questioned
but not its duration. The dead, one assumes, would not
mind attaining a homeless status, and sleep in archways
or watch pregnant submarines returning
to their native pen after a worldwide journey
without destroying life on earth, without
even a proper flag to hoist.

1992

DAEDALUS IN SICILY

All his life he was building something, inventing something.
Now, for a Cretan queen, an artificial heifer,
so as to cuckold the king. Then a labyrinth, this time for
the king himself, to hide from bewildered glances
an unbearable offspring. Or a flying contraption, when
the king figured out in the end who it was at his court
who was keeping himself so busy with new commissions.
The son on that journey perished falling into the sea,
like Phaeton, who, they say, also spurned his father's
orders. Here, in Sicily, stiff on its scorching sand,
sits a very old man, capable of transporting
himself through the air, if robbed of other means of passage.
All his life he was building something, inventing something.
All his life from those clever constructions, from those inventions,
he had to flee. As though inventions
and constructions are anxious to rid themselves of their blueprints
like children ashamed of their parents. Presumably, that's the fear
of replication. Waves are running onto the sand;
behind, shine the tusks of the local mountains.
Yet he had already invented, when he was young, the seesaw,
using the strong resemblance between motion and stasis.
The old man bends down, ties to his brittle ankle
(so as not to get lost) a lengthy thread,
straightens up with a grunt, and heads out for Hades.

1993
Translated by the author

CLOUDS

Ah, summer clouds
of the Baltic! I swear
you are nowhere
to be outclassed.

Isn't your free state
the afterworld's border—
stallions, a warrior,
sometimes a saint?

The Almighty alone
glimpses by lightning
your crumbling lining,
fraying cretonne.

Hence, I, an old
hand at premonitions,
take your omniscience
for non-being's mold,

afterlife's mask.
Steadily running
over the granite,
over the most

humble of seas,
you are the limpid
sculptures of limit-
less genesis.

Cupolas, peaks,
profile of Tolstoy,
muscular torso,
bachelor digs,

candlesticks' vain
meltdown, or Hapsburg
Vienna, an iceberg-
alias-brain,

Eden's debris.
Ah, save the northeaster,
you wouldn't master
geometry!

Your cirric ploys
or cumulous domus
make both the nomads
and the settled rejoice.

Thanks to your reams,
patches, and tatters,
words that one utters
equal one's dreams.

It's you who let
me with your nimbus
trust not in numbers
but in the complete

spurning of weights
and measures in favor
—once and forever—
of phantoms and grace.

It was you, too,
who made the salient
planet an island
paltry for two.

Ah, your rent-free
castles! Those lofty
soft hotbeds of the
heart's tyranny!

Frothy cascades
of seraphs and ball gowns;
crashing of bogus
starched barricades;

conjugal bouts
of butterflies and
the Himalayan
glaciers—ah, clouds,

high in pristine
skies of the Baltic!
Whose stern and vatic
calls have you been

heeding? To whose
might do you yield? Or
who is your builder?
Your Sisyphus?

Who, having found
shapes to your grandeur,
made it surrender
sound? For sound-

less is your great
miracle! Heavy
or scattered, your bevy,
cohort, parade

silently hedge
toward some finish
line, where you'll vanish
—toward the edge

etched by your shoal
that charged it more boldly,
and was lighter than body,
better than soul.

1989
Translated by the author

PORTRAIT OF TRAGEDY

Let's look at the face of tragedy. Let's see its creases,
its aquiline profile, its masculine jawbone. Let's hear its rhesus
contralto with its diabolic rises:
the aria of effect beats cause's wheezes.
How are you, tragedy? We haven't seen you lately.
Hello, the medal's flip side gone lazy.
Let's examine your aspects, lady.

Let's look into her eyes. Into her wide-with-senseless-
pain hazel pupils aimed like lenses
at us in the stalls, or touring in someone else's
predicament, on false pretenses.
Welcome, tragedy, with gods and heroes,
with the curtain exposing your feet, dirty with other eras,
with proper names sunk in the maddening chorus.

Let's put our fingers into her mouth that gnashes
scurvy-eaten keyboards inflamed by wolfram flashes
showing her spit-rich palate with blizzards of kinfolk's ashes.
Let's yank her hem, see if she blushes.
Well, tragedy, if you want, surprise us.
Show us a body betrayed or its demise, devices
for lost innocence, inner crisis.

Ah, but to press ourselves against her cheek, her Gorgon
coiling hairdo! Against the golden
icon's coarse wooden backside that hoards the burden
of proof the better the more her horizons broaden.
Greetings, tragedy, dressed slightly out of fashion,
with lengthy sentences making time look ashen.
Though you feel fine alfresco, it's the morgue you've got a crush on.

Let's tumble into her arms with a lecher's ardor!
Let's drown in her flabby rubble; yes, let's go under.
Let's burrow through her and make mattress fodder.
Who knows, she may carry. A race always needs a founder.
What's new on the schedule, tragedy, in your cartridge?
And re stuffing wombs, what takes more courage
to star in: a scene of carnage or a pile of garbage?

Ah, to inhale her stench of armpits and feces
mixed with the incense clouding subtracted faces;
to exclaim hysterically, You save this
for the sissies! And throw up into her laces.
Thanks, tragedy, for your attempts to cheer up
(since there is no abortion without a cherub),
for jackboots kicking the groin as though it's a stirrup.

Her face is abominable! It's never hidden
by the domino, makeup, duckweed, by heathen
ignorance, or by a fishnet mitten
involved in a stormy ovation, completely smitten.
Thanks, tragedy, for playing decent.
For being direct like a bullet, albeit distant.
For not wasting time, for happening in an instant.

Who are we, after all, neither oils nor statues,
not to allow the mangling of our lives as much as
one wishes? Which, too, could be seen as a boon. The catch is,
a thing must become unpalpable to look matchless.
Don't spurn that, tragedy, the genre of martyrs!
How about the loss of all that's sacred to us for starters?
Small wonder that togas become you as much as tatters.

Look at her, she is scowling! She says, "Good evening,
let me begin. In this business, folks, the beginning
matters more than the end. Give me a human being
and I'll begin with misfortune, so set the wristwatch for grieving."
Go ahead, tragedy! Among our vowels,
pick out the *yi*, born in the Mongol bowels,
and turn it, ripping our gushing ovals,

into a noun, a verb, an adjective! *yi*, our common gargle!
yi, we barf out as our gains and our losses ogle
us, or as we storm the exit. But there, an ogre,
you're looming large with your oblong cudgel and bulging goggle!
Tragedy, hit us like a relative. Make clowns of us.
Knead us into a pulp on our bunks and sofas.
Spit into our souls till you find a surface,

and afterwards also! Make it a swamp, and stir it,
so that neither the Father and Son nor the Holy Spirit
will clear it up. Curdle it into the serried
rubble. Plant there aspens, shoot up acid, and leave needles buried.
Let soul be like nature, tragedy; that won't wear badly.
Let's graft a seraph to the night-work buggy.
As the fruit told the botanist, Fine, make me ugly.

Once you were, dear, a beauty, a power, a non-stop torrent.
You'd come after midnight and flash a warrant.
You were quoting Racine; obscene you weren't.
Now you are the perspective stewed in the dead end. A worried
herd, though, finds its address, and a lamb an oven
by spotting your footprint that's fresh and cloven.
Come on! Fly the gates of your pigsty open.

1991
Translated by the author

TÖRNFALLET

There is a meadow in Sweden
where I lie smitten,
eyes stained with clouds'
white ins and outs.

And about that meadow
roams my widow
plaiting a clover
wreath for her lover.

I took her in marriage
in a granite parish.
The snow lent her whiteness,
a pine was a witness.

She'd swim in the oval
lake whose opal
mirror, framed by bracken,
felt happy broken.

And at night the stubborn
sun of her auburn
hair shone from my pillow
at post and pillar.

Now in the distance
I hear her descant.
She sings "Blue Swallow,"
but I can't follow.

The evening shadow
robs the meadow
of width and color.
It's getting colder.

As I lie dying
here, I'm eyeing
stars. Here's Venus;
no one between us.

1990/1993

Sunset clings to the samovar, abandoning the veranda,
but the tea has gone cold, or is finished; a fly scales a saucer's *dolce*.
And her heavy chignon makes Varvara Andreevna look grander
than ever. Her starched cotton blouse is staunchly
buttoned up to her chin. Vialtsev, deep in his chair, is nodding
over the rustling weekly with Dubrovo's latest swing
at the Cabinet. Varvara Andreevna under her skirts wears not a
thing.

The drawing room's dark piano responds to a dry ovation
of hawthorns. The student Maximov's few random chords
stir the garden's cicadas. In the platinum sky, athwart,
squadrons of ducks, foreshadowing aviation,
drift toward Germany. Hiding in the unlit
library, Dunia devours Nikki's letter, so full of cavils.
No looker; but, boy, what anatomy! And so unlike
hardcovers.

That is why Erlich winces, called in by Kartashov
to join Prigozhin, the doctor, and him at cards. "With pleasure."
Ah, but swatting a fly is simpler than staving off
a reverie of your niece, naked upon the leather
couch and fighting mosquitoes, fighting heat—but to no avail.
Prigozhin deals as he eats: with his belly virtually
crushing the flimsy table. Can the doctor be asked about this little boil?
Perhaps eventually.

Oppressive midsummer twilight; a truly myopic part
of day, when each shape and form loses resolve, gets eerily
vague. "In your linen suit, Piotr Lvovich, it's not so hard
to take you for one of the statues down in the alley." "Really?"
Erlich feigns embarrassment, rubbing his pince-nez's rim.
It's true, though: the far-off in twilight looks near, the near, alien;
and Erlich tries to recall how often he had Natalia
Fiodorovna in his dream.

But does Varvara Andreevna love the doctor? Gnarled poplars crowd
the dacha's wide-open windows with peasant-like abandon.
They are the ones to be asked: their branches, their crow-filled crowns.
Particularly, the elm climbing into Varvara's bedroom:
it alone sees the hostess with just her stockings on.
Outside, Dunia calls for a swim in the night lake: "Come, lazies!"
To leap! overturning the tables! Hard, though, if you are the one
with aces.

And the cicada chorus, with the strength of the stars' display,
burgeons over the garden, sounding like their utterance.
Which is, perhaps, the case. Where am I, anyway?
wonders Erlich, undoing his braces at the outhouse entrance.
It's twenty versts to the railroad. A rooster attempts its *lied*.
The student Maximov's pet word, interestingly, is "fallacy."
In the provinces, too, nobody's getting laid,
as throughout the galaxy.

1993 • *Translated by Jonathan Aaron with the author*

A TALE

In walks the Emperor, dressed as Mars;
    his medals clink and sway.
The General Staff sports so many stars,
    it looks like the Milky Way.

The Emperor says, "I guess you guess
    what you are here for."
The generals rise and bark, "Oh yes,
    Sire! To start a war."

"Right," says the Emperor. "Our enemy
    is powerful, mean, and brash.
But we'll administer him such an enema
    his toilet won't need a flush.

"Move your artillery! Move your warships!
    Where is my gorgeous horse?
Forward! May God, whom our nation worships,
    join our brave air force!"

"Yes!" cry the warriors. "Our job is carnage,
    ruin, destruction, void.
We promise, Sire: we'll find a Carthage
    and we'll leave it destroyed."

"Great!" cries the Emperor. "What one conquers
    is up to the scholars' quills.
And let the Treasury boys go bonkers
    trying to pay the bills."

The generals thunder: "Well said, Sire.
    Our coin is of tolling bells.
May the sun that won't set over your empire
    rise for nobody else!"

And off roars the turbine, off clangs the metal,
    off they march, hand on hilt,
as many a rose curls its tender petal
    ready to wait and wilt.

II

It's no Armageddon, it's not some smarmy
    earthquake or H-bomb test.
No, it's just the Imperial Army
    trying to do its best.

The sky is falling, the earth is gaping,
    the ocean simply boils.
"Life," says the Emperor, "is just aping
    popular abstract oils.

"War," he continues, "is like a museum."
　　And the Top Brass agree:
"Sire, we'll paint like that ad nauseam,
　　since Art equals History!

"History never says it's sorry,
　　nor does it say, What if.
To enter History, a territory
　　first has to come to grief."

"History never says it's sorry,"
　　join the enlisted men.
"Who needs memento when we've got mori?
　　History must know when."

"Ah, tell them to turn the good old horizon
　　vertical, save its sail,"
adds the Emperor, with his eyes on
　　the most minute detail.

"Yes," cry the generals. "Yes, for heaven's
　　sake. That's what's been amiss.
Let's push the button and see what happens.
　　This must be a masterpiece."

And lo, the world turns topsy-turvy,
    in other words, goes bust.
"Gosh," says the Emperor. "That was nervy,
    but, in the context, just."

III

Now there's nothing around to argue
    over: no pros or cons.
"Hey, enemy!" the Emperor shouts. "Are you
    there?"—There's no response.

Now it's pure space, devoid of mountains,
    plains, and their bric-a-brac.
"Let's," says the Emperor, "sing our anthem's
    lyrics and raise the flag."

Up flies the pennant, attended only
    by two or three evening bats.
"A victory often makes one lonely,"
    the Emperor says, then adds:

"Let's have a monument, since my stallion,
    white as a hyacinth,
is old and looks, as it were, quite alien;
    and write on the granite plinth:

""'Tight was the enemy's precious anus.
        We, though, stood strong and firm.'
The critics might say that we went bananas.
        But we've got it all on film.

"Lest her sweet mutants still cry, the mother
        may sing them the ancient lay.
The future as such has no purpose, other
        than pushing down Replay."

At sunset, everything looks quite pretty.
        Down goes the temperature.
The world lies motionless, like a treaty
        without a signature.

The stars start to twinkle, remote and jolly.
        The eye travels rather far.
One feels a little bit melancholy.
        But there is one's cigar.

                                                        1995

VIEW WITH A FLOOD

A somewhat familiar landscape, currently flooded. Currently
it's only cupolas, spires, treetops, a rainy gauze.
The throat wells up with a gurgling, passionate commentary,
but out of the bunch of words all that remains is was.

That's how, toward the end, a mirror reflects a veteran's
baldness, but not his face, let alone his butt.
Below, sheer washed-out scribblings and swallowed utterance.
Above, the snatch of a cloud. And you stand in water. Cut.

It seems the scene is somewhere in the Netherlands; very probably
prior to their having dikes, and names like Van Dam, De Vries.
Or else it's Southeast Asia, with the monsoon soberly
softening up the paddies. But you are no rice.

Clearly it rose drop by drop, for years, attempting a neverscape
whose potable swells now crave new distances: salty, vast.
And it's high time to shoulder the child like a periscope
to spot the faraway enemy battleships steaming fast.

1993
Translated by the author

ISCHIA IN OCTOBER

TO FAUSTO MALCOVATI

Once a volcano here belched with zest.
Later, a pelican plucked its breast.
Virgil dwelt not too far away,
and Wystan Auden held drinks at bay.

These days, the palaces' stucco peels,
frightful prices make longer bills.
Yet I somehow still make, amid
all these changes, my line ends meet.

A fisherman sails into the azure,
away from the drying bed linen's lure.
And autumn splashes the mountain ridge
with a wave unknown to the empty beach.

On the balustrade, my wife and child
peer at a distant piano lid
of sail, or at the small balloon
of Angelus fleeing the afternoon.

Unreachable, as it were, by foot,
an island as a kind of fate
suits solely the sirocco; but
we also are fluent at

banging the shutters. A sudden draft
scattering papers right and left
is proof that in this limestone
place we are not alone.

The rectangular, mortal-held eggshell,
enduring the wind's solid brow, as well
as the breakers' wet hammer works,
reveals at dusk three yolks.

The bougainvillea's tightly wound
scrawl helps the isolated ground
to shade its limited shame a bit,
avenging thus space with writ.

Almost no people; so that pronouns
sharpen one's features all at once,
as though speech makes them definite like a lens
at the vista's expense.

And should someone sigh longingly "Home," your hand
more willingly than to the continent
might point to the cumulous peaks where great
worlds rise and disintegrate.

We are a threesome here and I bet
what we together are looking at
is three times more addressless and more blue
than what Aeneas saw sailing through.

1993

Translated by the author

IN FRONT OF CASA MARCELLO

The sun's setting, and the corner bar bangs its shutters.
Lampposts flare up, as though an actress

paints her eyelids dark violet, looking both rum and scary.
And the headache is parachuting squarely

behind enemy wrinkles. While five enormous
pigeons on the Palazzo Minelli's cornice

are copulating in the last rays of sunset,
paying no heed, as our Stone Age ancest-

ors did, no doubt, to their scruffy neighbors,
already asleep or a little nervous.

The booming bells of the slant bell tower
rooted in the ultramarine sky over

this town are like fruits keen on falling rather
than hitting the ground. If there is another

life, someone picks them up there. Well, pretty
soon we'll find out. Here, where plenty

of saliva, rapturous tears, and even
seed has been shed, in a nook of the earthly Eden,

I stand in the evening, absorbing slowly
with the dirty sponge of my lungs the lovely,

transparent, autumn-*cum*-winter, lucent
local oxygen, pink with loosened

tiles and a windowsill's carnation,
and giving the scent of cells' liberation

from time. The money-like, crumpled water
of the canal, buying off the palazzo's outer

riches, ends up with a somewhat shady,
peeling-off deal that includes a shaky

caryatid shouldering still the organ
of speech, with its cigarette, and ogling

the scenes, breathtaking for their oblivion
of propriety, happening in the avian

bedroom, exposed to a passing party,
and resembling now a windswept palm tree,

now a jumble of numerals insane with their quest for timing,
now a line scrawled in haste and rhyming.

1995 • *Translated by the author*

REVEILLE

Birds acquaint themselves with leaves.
Hired hands roll up their sleeves.
In a brick malodorous dorm
boys awake awash in sperm.

Clouds of patently absurd
but endearing shapes assert
the resemblance of their lot
to a cumulative thought.

As the sun displays its badge
to the guilty world at large,
scruffy masses have to rise,
unless ordered otherwise.

Now let's see what one can't see
elsewhere in the galaxy:
life on earth, of which its press
makes a lot and comets less.

As a picture doomed to sneak
previews only, it's unique
even though some action must
leave its audience aghast.

Still, the surplus of the blue
up on high supplies a clue
as to why our moral laws
won't receive their due applause.

What we used to blame on gods
now gets chalked up to the odds
of small particles whose sum
makes you miss the older sham.

Yet regardless of the cause,
or effects that make one pause,
one is glad that one has been
caught this morning in between.

Painted by a gentle dawn
one is proud that like one's own
planet now one will not wince
at what one is facing, since

putting up with nothing whose
company we cannot lose
hardens rocks and—rather fast—
hearts as well. But rocks will last.

1996

TO MY DAUGHTER

Give me another life, and I'll be singing
in Caffè Rafaella. Or simply sitting
there. Or standing there, as furniture in the corner,
in case that life is a bit less generous than the former.

Yet partly because no century from now on will ever manage
without caffeine or jazz, I'll sustain this damage,
and through my cracks and pores, varnish and dust all over,
observe you, in twenty years, in your full flower.

On the whole, bear in mind that I'll be around. Or rather,
that an inanimate object might be your father,
especially if the objects are older than you, or larger.
So keep an eye on them always, for they no doubt will judge you.

Love those things anyway, encounter or no encounter.
Besides, you may still remember a silhouette, a contour,
while I'll lose even that, along with the other luggage.
Hence, these somewhat wooden lines in our common language.

1994

MCMXCV

The clowns are demolishing the circus. The elephants have run off
    to India;
tigers sell, on the sidewalk, their stripes and hoops;
under the leaky cupola, there is hanging, off the trapeze,
as in a wardrobe, the limp tuxedo
of a disillusioned magician;
and little horses, casting off their embroidered blankets, pose
for a portrait of the new engine. In the arena,
knee-deep in sawdust, clowns, wildly wielding
sledgehammers, demolish the circus.
The public is either absent or doesn't clap.
Only a miniature shaggy poodle
still yelps incessantly, feeling she's getting closer
to her sugar lump: feeling that any second
she'll be hitting nineteen ninety-five.

1995

Translated by the author

FLOURISH

O if the birds sang while the clouds felt bored by singing,
and the eye gaining blue as it traced their trill
could make out the keys in the door and, beyond, a ceiling,
and those whose address at present begins with nil.

And other than that, it's just shifting of chairs and sofas,
and flowers on walls and in vases obstruct their view.
And if there was ever a bee sans beehive or solace
with extra spores on its paws, it's you.

O if the transparent things in their blue garret
could hold their eye-dodging matter in second gear
to curdle themselves one day into a tear or star at
this end of the universe. Afterwards, everywhere.

Yet oxygen seems to be just the raw material
for lace strung out on spokes in the tsars' back yard,
and the statues freeze as though they smell a serial
Decembrist, beheaded later and breathing hard.

1994
Translated by the author

TAPS

I've been reproached for everything save the weather
and in turn my own neck was seeking a scimitar.
But soon, I'm told, I'll lose my epaulets altogether
and dwindle into a little star.

I'll twinkle among the wires, a sky's lieutenant,
and hide in clouds when thunder roars,
blind to the troops as they fold their pennant
and run, pursued by the pen, in droves.

With nothing around to care for, it's of no import
if you are blitzed, encircled, reduced to nil.
Thus wetting his dream with the tumbled ink pot,
a schoolboy can multiply as no tables will.

And although the speed of light can't in nature covet
thanks, non-being's blue armor plate,
prizing attempts at making a sifter of it,
might use my pinhole, at any rate.

1994

Translated by the author

INDEX OF TITLES AND FIRST LINES